RADIO

RADIO

MAKING WAVES IN SOUND

ALASDAIR PINKERTON

REAKTION BOOKS
*Published in association with
the Science Museum, London*

For Philippa

Published by Reaktion Books Ltd
Unit 32, Waterside
44–48 Wharf Road
London N1 7UX, UK
www.reaktionbooks.co.uk

In association with the Science Museum
Exhibition Road
London SW7 2DD, UK
www.sciencemuseum.org.uk

First published 2019

Printed and bound in China by 1010 Printing International Ltd

A catalogue record for this book is available from the British Library

ISBN 978 1 78914 078 1

CONTENTS

An American dairy farmer in 1923 tunes the radio, headphones on, as he prepares for milking.

INTRODUCTION: MYTHOLOGY AND MAGNETISM

R adio is a medium of seemingly endless contradictions. It is the world's most ubiquitous means of mass communication but so ephemeral that the greater part of its broadcast history has faded from the historical archive; constructive of enormous global audiences but also of intensely personal and intimate communication; capable of eliciting feelings of friendship and community but also of fear, loathing and even hatred. It is a technology that is now in its third century of existence but continues to resound with startlingly modern ambitions and evolve and flourish, despite frequent predictions of demise, in the age of the Internet and social media. Radio is a technology that has fundamentally changed the way the world works and has ushered in a new era of electronic communications, but today it is taken almost entirely for granted.

As we shall explore, radio is the subject of enormous interest, intrigue, ignorance and no shortage of mythology. Its history is enriched with tales of heroes and villains, virtuous acts, deceits, double-crossing and generally despicable behaviours. Like the great myths from human history, radio's mythologies are subject to constant reinterpretation. Contemporary judgements about the heroism or villainy of radio's early protagonists are shaped by our willingness to believe in the 'how?', 'why?' and 'where?' of particular acts of inventiveness, the presence of 'genius' or the mastery of publicity, and faith in radio's particular 'national' narratives. This all seems highly appropriate for

RADIO
and Television
TODAY
BBC LONDON CALLING
GIRL OF MY DREAMS
THE SCORE IS NOW 7 TO 6
Callahan
SELL 'EM
RADIO....MUSIC....
FOR EVERYBODY!
SEPTEMBER

Hans Thoma
(1839–1910), *Jupiter*,
colour lithograph.

the story of a natural physical phenomenon that can be traced to the
moment of creation.

For many thousands of years, human civilization has pursued philosophical enquiry into the nature, the substance and the meaning of two
seemingly unconnected phenomena: electricity and magnetism. These
forces, these energies, inspired investigation and intrigue throughout
the ancient and modern worlds of mythology, natural philosophy
and science. Control over the elements was rooted in the myths and
teachings of ancient Greece. Electricity's most violent manifestation,

Selling a vision for
radio's invasion of
the home in *Radio
and Television Today*,
September 1940.

lightning, was attributed to Zeus, the son of Chronos and brother to Poseidon and Hades, as a gift for freeing the three Cyclopes from the dungeon prison of Tartarus. Somewhat later Zeus, following a certain clash with the Titans, would go on to win control over the medium through which his great power moved and was manifest: the air and sky. Zeus' equivalent in Roman mythology was perhaps even more poetic. According to the theologian Georg Wissowa, the Roman god Jupiter came to assume almost atmospheric qualities as the wielder of lightning and master of the weather. But this was not to suggest that Jupiter was too elevated, too heavenly or too naturalistic. Jupiter's watchful vigilance over earthly events led to a belief that he was also a guardian of public oaths and a guarantor of good faith, roles which could only be achieved through a capacity to communicate between the heavens and the Earth, between the gods and mankind. Throughout the Roman world, it was Jupiter's command of atmospheric electricity – lightning – and its sonic rebound – thunder – that were held up as the *ex caelo* (from the sky) conductors of this heavenly communication.

Such interpretations were not without challenge in the ancient world. The scientific revolution that began in Ionia during the sixth century BC provoked philosophical reflection on both electricity and magnetism, including that of Anaximander of Miletus (*c.* 610–546 BC), who attributed thunder and lightning not to the gods but to the interaction of physical and atmospheric elements. In this case, thunder and lightning were considered to be the burning fires sparked by clouds hitting one another with varying degrees of force. For Anaxagoras (*c.* 500–428 BC), the same fires were provoked by the combustible upper ether descending into the lower atmosphere, whereas for Empedocles (*c.* 490–430 BC) fire was provoked by the sun's rays becoming trapped within the cloud formations. Aristotle (*c.* 384–322 BC), too, subscribed to the fire theory, although he was dismissive of previous theorizations that attempted to explain thunder as the sound of the fires hissing when quenched. Notwithstanding their distinctly pre-modern registers, these various ideas were part of a discernible attempt to understand and interpret the phenomenon of lightning and the structure of the air and atmosphere that spawned it. With his eyes more closely trained to the ground, the Greek philosopher and mathematician Thales of Miletus (624–546 BC) is credited with discovering that amber, when rubbed with fur, produces a force that attracts smaller and lighter objects – such as dust or grass – towards it. He observed a similar phenomenon with a lodestone and pieces of iron. Although Thales had eschewed all gods and theistic forces and looked instead to nature for an explanation, he could not have known that he was observing the effects of both static electricity and magnetism – two related but very different kinds of forces – at work.

That relationship wouldn't be demonstrated theoretically until the publication of James Clerk Maxwell's seminal *A Dynamical Theory of the Electromagnetic Field* in 1865. And yet Thales, Anaximander and others had started on a path of investigation into two hidden, unseen and unknown forces that influenced and governed the world around them, and which continue to govern the world around us. By thinking about the constitution of lightning, the Greek natural philosophers were also forced into considering the composition of the air and atmosphere within which lightning was contained, and through which it was transmitted. The story of electromagnetism and the discovery of radio almost two millennia later provoked, as we will see, a similar attempt to sort out the air, the atmosphere and human misunderstandings of their composition.

What follows in this book is a story of our very human relationship with radio – a story that traces radio's technological, political, social and cultural emergence from experimental laboratories of Victorian science to become a near-ubiquitous presence in our everyday lives. The book is shaped by radio's multiple characters and characteristics: a natural phenomenon, but one that has been harnessed and moulded by human beings to bridge oceans and reconfigure our experience of time and space – and which, today, has the capacity to enthuse, entertain, entice and enrage in equal measure. Such is the complexity of radio, this book draws on primary research and accounts that go well beyond my areas of specialist knowledge in geography and politics. Each chapter, though, does seek to explore a different dimension of radio's interrelationship with the human world: charting its extent, its limits and its extremes; the multiple genealogies of radio's discovery and its embrace as a communications technology; radio's capacity to build and shape communities in the air and on the ground; as an international phenomenon and instrument of governance; radio's implication in war and the battle for human minds; and, finally, tracing radio's appearance in the very human world of popular culture.

The purpose here is not to present a complete (or even abridged) account of the rich interdisciplinary literatures through which radio has been discussed and debated. Rather, like radio itself, my path through this world of radio knowledge has been oscillatory – weaving and meandering from technical accounts of radio propagation characteristics, patent filings and technical drawings, to novels, poems and paintings that treat radio as either the subject or object of their attention. In turning these movements into chapters, there has been some inevitable blurring and overlapping around the margins – not so much interference (I hope) as a recognition that radio exists on a continuous spectrum and that any attempt at partitioning will be necessarily artificial.

WHAT IS RADIO?

Radio waves are not all the same – the product of both manmade and entirely natural sources and displaying behaviours within the Earth's atmosphere that are far from uniform. All this begs the question, what *is* radio?

At its most elemental, radio refers to the transmission, or radiation, of electromagnetic energy through space. As with all classifications of electromagnetic energy, including heat and light, radio travels in the form of an oscillating wave – although unlike visible light, radio waves

Ecko radios featured large dials for selecting international radio stations, as seen at Radiolympia, London, 1938.

can't be seen by the human eye. Radio waves are longer and oscillate more slowly (that is, at a lower frequency) than visible light, although they travel at the same speed as light – approximately 300,000 km (186,000 mi.) per second. Light waves oscillate at between 430 and 790 terahertz (THz) (that is, 790 trillion cycles per second), whereas radio waves oscillate within the rather more pedestrian range of 3 gigahertz (GHz) (3 billion cycles per second) and 3 kilohertz (kHz) (3,000 cycles per second). The wavelengths of light are usually stated as being in the range of 400–700 nanometres (that is, billionths of a metre), whereas radio waves are much longer, ranging in length from about 1 mm to more than 100 km (³⁄₆₄ in. to 62 mi.).

These numbers are both overwhelmingly large and small and bear little relationship to our understanding of the world on a human scale. They are, though, critical in determining the position of radio waves on the electromagnetic spectrum (the complete range of different forms of electromagnetic energy) and in understanding the ways in which radio waves interact with the physical environment on Earth and beyond our own atmosphere. The distinct frequencies and wavelengths of radio waves may prevent their detection by the sensory organs of human beings, but it is these same distinctive characteristics that have made radio waves such an important part of modern human communication.

Just as the waves that, together, constitute visible light are considered to be a distinct portion of the much wider electromagnetic spectrum, so too is the 'radio spectrum'. Some radio waves have a comparatively long wavelength and others comparatively short. Radio waves with the longest wavelengths have the lowest frequency, whereas those with the shortest wavelength have the highest frequency. The International Telecommunication Union (ITU) divides the radio spectrum into nine categories – or bands – of radio waves, ranging from 'Tremendously High Frequency', or THF, through to 'Tremendously Low Frequency', or TLF. The radio waves used for most commercial applications of radio form only a very small part of this broader spectrum. The radio waves that are used for the most popular music and speech radio stations around the world, for example, are commonly within the so-called 'VHF' or 'Very High Frequency' band and tend to cluster around the 100 MHz spot on our radio dials or displays. In Los Angeles, the hugely popular KISS-FM broadcasts across the city on 102.7 MHz. In the Pacific northwest of the U.S., KEXP broadcasts on 90.3 MHz from its headquarters in Seattle, Washington. The UK's most popular radio station, BBC Radio 2, occupies a range of frequencies from 88–91 MHz for listeners across the British Isles, while in India, Radio Mirchi broadcasts on 98.3 MHz to audiences in 33 cities across the subcontinent. At this frequency, radio waves have a wavelength of about 3 m (9¾ ft) and have desirable characteristics for broadcasting high-quality music and speech programming. VHF waves are less affected by 'atmospheric noise' and interference from electrical equipment than lower frequencies, and are relatively unaffected by buildings and, crucially, can be received indoors.

VHF waves propagate – that is to say they *travel* – chiefly along a straight line of sight and cannot, in general, travel over the horizon. With careful positioning on hilltops, and with tall masts that can raise radio transmitters several hundred metres into the air (thus increasing the distance of the so called 'radio horizon'), VHF may achieve a broadcast radius of about 160 km (100 mi.) With such small broadcast footprints, multiple VHF transmitters are required to achieve a reasonable level of coverage even in the smallest of countries. In the UK, for example, the BBC requires 39 separate transmitter stations, situated throughout Great Britain, Northern Ireland and the Scottish Islands in order to achieve something close to 'national' coverage for their VHF radio services. Medium Frequency – or medium wave (MW) – transmissions have a wider broadcast footprint than VHF waves. They can follow the curvature of the Earth over the horizon, are capable of diffracting over hills and can travel for several hundred kilometres from the originating transmitter mast – and even further than that if travelling over water or water-saturated ground.

Unlike VHF waves, medium waves are also capable of so-called skywave propagation – a process by which radio waves of particular wavelengths and frequencies can be made to travel great distances by reflecting and refracting between the Earth's surface and the ionosphere (a layer of the atmosphere ionized by the sun's radiation) in a planetary-scale skipping motion. Short waves (waves of less than 200 m/656 ft in length) are perhaps the most well-known utilizers of skywave propagation and, as a result, are capable of travelling many thousands of kilometres to almost any point on the surface of the Earth. International broadcasting organizations such as the Voice of America (VOA) and the BBC World Service use just this kind of propagation technique in order to 'skip' signals deep into territories where radio signals might otherwise be absent or local radio infrastructure may be limited. Broadcasting of this kind is far from straightforward for either the broadcaster or the listener. It doesn't simply require powerful and highly directional transmitter stations, or listeners with large aerial arrays, but also the cooperation of a turbulent and constantly changing ionosphere – the refractive qualities of which change diurnally (that is, from day to night), seasonally and in response to solar activity (such as solar flares).

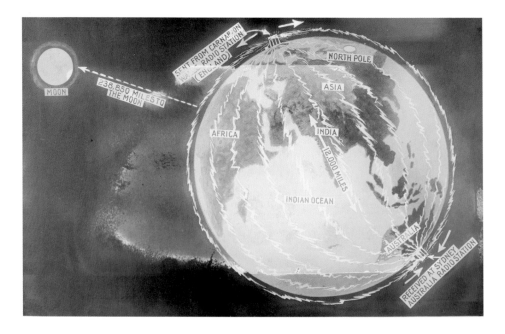

As well as being divided into nine distinct 'bands', the ITU also divides the radio spectrum for the use of more than forty 'radiocommunication services' by attempting to match the technical requirements of the particular 'service' to the technical characteristics of the different frequency bands. Within this internationally agreed framework, national governments are then able to apportion their 'national spectrum' for specific functions in the hope of maximizing the capacity of the spectrum while avoiding potentially harmful interference between services. In the United States, for example, the 390 MHz frequency is commonly used for remotely controlled garage doors and alarm systems and 900 MHz for domestic cordless phones; whereas, at the other end of the scale, Air Traffic Control radar operates between 960 and 1,215 MHz and GPS 'sat navs' between 1.2 and 1.7 GHz. Even in this globally and nationally regulated environment, unintended radio interference can still take place. When the U.S. military began an $800 million upgrade to its radio communications equipment during the so-called Global War on Terror, for example, reports started to appear from across the

Connecting the world via shortwave radio: a wall poster from the U.S. National Radio School, *c.* 1919.

continental U.S. that something was interfering with that great symbol of American technological freedom – the remote-controlled garage opener. It turned out that the military's new 'state-of-the-art' Land Mobile Radio System (LMRS) utilizes radio frequencies between 380 and 399.9 MHz, including the 390 MHz frequency used by garage-door openers. This placed the demands of 'national security' in a direct, if unintended, electromagnetic challenge with the domestic security of many American homeowners who found their garage doors taking on a life of their own – opening and closing at will and failing to respond to their remote clickers. Newspaper headline writers across the U.S. – from Los Angeles to Florida, Georgia and Washington, DC – went with the theme of garage doors 'only following military orders' or doing 'battle' with the military's new systems in what were 'open and shut' cases. Estimates suggest that some 50 million garage-door systems were affected and required reprogramming by this 'military assault', but the

The Solar Flare Effect (SFE) on the ionosphere can cause radio blackouts.

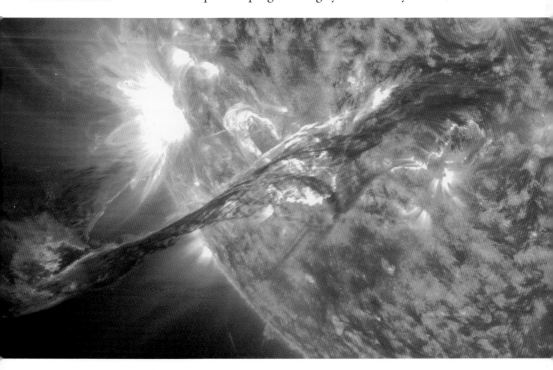

reality is more complex than the headlines. The U.S. Department of Defense had owned the 380–99 MHz spectrum within the continental United States since the 1950s but had not routinely used these frequencies until the rollout of LMRS from 2004. Manufacturers of electric garage doors, on the other hand, have used the 390 MHz frequency for their controller units since the early 1980s, as permitted under U.S. law, believing it to be a 'good frequency' for garage-door openers because transmissions can penetrate the metal doors. For the military, access to these frequencies will allow high-quality voice and data transmissions across the U.S., but this particular conflict is ultimately the product of increased demand for space on a radio spectrum that is becoming congested with military and commercial communications, data and signals.

Such is the demand for the radio spectrum, it has become common around the world for national governments to auction off sections of the spectrum to companies who wish to develop services that utilize radio waves of particular frequencies. Successive British governments have enjoyed enormous windfalls when auctioning parts of the radio spectrum for new-generation mobile phone services. The most lucrative of these auctions was held in the UK between 6 March and 27 April 2000, when '3G' was at the cutting edge of mobile phone services, promising faster and more extensive coverage for data transfer than had ever before been possible. In a little under two months of bidding and counter-bidding for one of five 3G licences, the British government scooped a reward of £22.5 billion from the likes of Vodafone and other mobile phone companies in what was widely acclaimed to be the world's 'biggest-ever' auction. 'Not since the Praetorian Guard knocked down the entire Roman Empire to Didius Julianus in AD 195 had there been an auction quite as large,' claimed the auction's designers and operators, although the subsequent auction held by the German government in July–August 2000 secured an even more impressive €50.8 billion.[1]

1
WIRELESS WORLDS

R adio has been described as the 'everywhere' medium.[1] It is the world's
most ubiquitous means of mass communication. It surrounds us
almost every minute of every day, carried through the air from transmitter masts to the most remote places on Earth and even beyond our
own atmosphere. It has a global audience of millions – even billions
– located everywhere from the most advanced and developed cities in
the Global North to the poorest communities in the developing world.
Radios are relatively cheap to buy or build (although they can also be
very expensive indeed) and unlike television, which has traditionally
been consumed in a fixed place within the home, radio is a remarkably
mobile accompaniment to our daily lives. We listen in our cars as we
travel to and from the workplace, at our desks and on the factory floor,
and on personal devices as we cycle, walk or go running. We listen
within sports arenas, in the garden, and in the kitchen as we prepare
the evening meal. For many, radio is the first thing they hear in the
morning and the last thing they hear before falling asleep at night. The
world over, radio's messages drift on the air from open car windows and
shop doorways in momentary competition, occupying our soundscapes
and connecting us briefly with familiar and unfamiliar radio worlds.
Radio brings us our daily news, music of every conceivable variety,
comedy and drama, but equally may deliver essential information about
maritime conditions, crop reports, immunization programmes or the
location of essential food supplies. Radio has the capacity to support

The UN distributes radios to support returning communities in Darfur, Sudan, in 2012.

in times of plenty and sustain in moments of crisis. It is, for many, a 'portable friend'.

From the moment that radio waves were first harnessed to carry messages through the air during the late nineteenth century, their capacity to traverse space and to bring people and places into close contact intrigued, fascinated and was widely celebrated. The widely acknowledged father of long-distance radio communications, Guglielmo Marconi (1874–1937), was particularly attuned to the geographical opportunities of these burgeoning technologies. Marconi was, first and foremost, an entrepreneur set on exploiting the commercial and military opportunities that would come from enhanced ship-to-ship and ship-to-shore communications. Nonetheless, he also displayed an almost missionary zeal in the quest to 'annihilate' space and time, and to defeat the strictures of distance. It was Marconi's obsession with the bridging of oceans by electromagnetic means that drove his investment into ever more powerful transmitting stations on both sides of the Atlantic Ocean during the early 1900s, including the Marconi stations near Poldhu in Cornwall (1901) and Caernarfon in North Wales (1914) and, correspondingly, transmitter stations near St John's, Newfoundland

and the New Brunswick Marconi Station in the U.S. state of New Jersey
(1913). Other stations dotted the coastlines of Canada, the United
States, Ireland and the United Kingdom in order to create multiple
points of connection across the Atlantic. Marconi's single-mindedness
was not without its casualties or controversies, and yet no one played
a more important part in shaping the radio's early iconography. Radio
was to be consumed on a gargantuan scale – from the power it consumed and the physical size of its engineering and infrastructure, to
the global reach of its message. In much the same way as the tea clipper,
the steamship and telegraph cable had accelerated communications
during the course of the nineteenth century, radio was bound up in a
glorious technological project to bring distant points on the Earth's
surface into close, even immediate, contact.

But if radio has become 'the everywhere medium' it also remains
'somewhere', rooted in place and reliant on (even interdependent
with) specific sites of production, transmission, relay and reception.
In a world that is increasingly littered with communications masts,
electricity pylons, mobile phone towers and other workaday bits of
apparatus, radio's infrastructure may often appear (or not appear at
all) as somewhat unremarkable features in our everyday lives – even
when that infrastructure is of historical or cultural importance. And
yet, some of radio's sites have acquired iconic status, entering popular
culture and public awareness, while others have the potential to reveal
something of radio's physical and geographical extremes.

LOCATING 'THE EVERYWHERE MEDIUM'

According to UNESCO, 95 per cent of the world's population (including
75 per cent of households in the developing world) are able to receive
radio broadcasts, and the vast majority of us come to know radio as
listeners to a range of local, national and possibly even international
radio stations. We are surrounded by radios. In the industrialized world,
there are 2.2 radio receivers for each individual person. That equates to

2.6 billion radio receivers owned by some 480 million households – with radio being accessible, at least statistically, to every man, woman and child. In the developing world, radio can be heard in almost all households that have an electricity supply, and an increasing number of households that don't, thanks to old and new technologies that can power radios using kinetic and renewable energy sources. There are, it is suggested, 0.2 radios per person (1.5 per household) in the developing world, an estimated total of 1.4 billion radio receivers and a total audience of 3.14 billion listeners.

Statistics reveal that in 1992 there were 576.5 million radios in the United States, split across nearly 97 million households; $2.6 billion was spent on the purchase of radio sets during that year alone. Radios can be found in 95 per cent of all cars and 172 million bedrooms across the United States – perhaps unsurprisingly given that radio receivers have been integrated into another great invention, the alarm clock, since the mid-1940s. More intriguingly, perhaps, 14.7 million American bathrooms contained a radio – a statistic that discloses rather more than we may care to know about the listening habits of a significant number of American citizens. While these statistics uncover something of the saturation of radio in the lives and homes of developed and developing world economies, they also represent a very particular understanding of radio. This is radio as a material commodity – an object that can be bought, sold or traded, placed on the shelves or in the showers of dwellings the world over.

But radio is much more than just a domestic appliance. Unlike with dishwashers or toasters, radio is both material and immaterial. It is at once that metal, wooden or plastic box that we intermittently interact with, but also something *extra*, something *more*. The radio set is, in itself, a somewhat worthless assembly of electronic components (albeit with an important history of invention and development); its real value comes from the capacity of those components to pluck signals out of the air and then turn them into something audible. Radio isn't therefore only an object, it is also a technology of transmission and reception that is itself built on systems, processes, infrastructures and networks of highly trained professionals – from engineers to producers and presenters – who are, in turn, subject to the priorities of commercial or public service broadcasters and, in most cases, strict regulations imposed by national government and international agreements. But even this doesn't begin to capture the complexity or diversity of radio as a spatial medium that has changed and challenged our experience of the modern world.

In the United States, 'national' radio broadcasting during the 1920s and 1930s became focused on New York City, with the emergence of the National Broadcasting Corporation and their occupation of a large portion of 30 Rockefeller Plaza, the centrepiece of the strikingly modern and Art Deco-styled Rockefeller Center when it was completed in 1933. Not only did NBC occupy eleven floors of the new Radio Corporation of America building (as it was then known), but their sound engineers worked in close collaboration with the building's architects to ensure that the new broadcasting facilities were truly state of the art and attuned to the specific requirements of a national radio broadcaster. Insulation and isolation were critical qualities. 'The studio complex was structurally isolated from the rest of the building', notes Emily Thompson, 'to prevent the transmission of noise and vibration. Each individual studio was further isolated to ensure a totally soundproof environment, and a quieted air-conditioning system ventilated the entire windowless complex.'[2] This was an architectural and engineering feat so singular in its devotion to radio and the sound medium that it came to be celebrated after its inauguration in purposefully sacred tones. Popular magazines of the day dubbed the studios a 'temple to glorify the radio voice' and a 'gigantic cathedral of sound'.[3] Others simply came to know it as New York's 'Radio City'. More than eighty years later and NBC still broadcasts live radio from the Rockefeller Center, although much of the studio space has been turned over to the production of live television shows, including the *Tonight Show* (the world's longest-running television talk show) and *Morning Joe* (MSNBC network). The importance of the Rockefeller Center site in the history and heritage

Radio City Music Hall in New York City is often referred to as the 'Showplace of the Nation'.

of U.S. radio (and vice versa) is not forgotten. Visitors taking the NBC studio tour will still see 'Radio City' on their tickets and radio's legacy is preserved in the official name of Rockefeller Center's internationally renowned entertainment venue, the Radio City Music Hall.

New York's Art Deco radio masterpiece was pre-empted by the BBC's own (if rather more modest) Art Deco headquarters – Broadcasting House on Portland Place in central London. The *Architectural Review* (1932) saw this building as 'a new Tower of London', whereas an inscription within the atrium proclaimed it to be 'a temple of the arts and muses'. This first purpose-built broadcasting facility in the United Kingdom continues to function as the corporation's headquarters and primary radio studio complex to the present day, having been overhauled and extended during a £1 billion redevelopment completed in 2013.[4]

Other iconic radio sites are less well preserved. The now-iconic Wardenclyffe Tower, designed by the Serbian American radio pioneer Nikola Tesla (1856–1943), was lost from the skyline of Shoreham, Long Island, in 1917 – demolished on the grounds of wartime 'national security'. Recent efforts to have the site designated as a U.S. national monument have so far failed to gain political support. The equally iconic hyperboloid structure of the Shabolovka Tower in central Moscow (designed by pioneering Russian architect Vladimir Shukhov, 1853–1939) nearly met a similar end when it was scheduled for demolition in 2014, only

Listening to an audition in the BBC's Broadcasting House, London, 10 March 1936.

for Moscow city authorities to grant a preservation notice following an international campaign to have it saved. In the absence of any restoration plans, the tower's long-term survival remains uncertain, although a 1:30 scale model of Shukhov's radio tower can now be seen in the Science Museum in London. These and other losses (or near-misses – hardly a trace remains of Marconi's pioneering radio infrastructures, for example) reveal something of the ongoing challenge to protect and conserve industrial and communications heritage, but, equally, a widespread inattentiveness to the critical importance of radio in our lives and landscapes.

Radio infrastructures are today only visible in the event of their sudden destruction. The loss of radio and television services across New York City at 10.28 a.m. on 11 September 2001, for example, was an agonizing audio-visual signal that the World Trade Center's

Nikola Tesla's Wardenclyffe Tower (built 1901, demolished 1917) in Shoreham, New York.

Radio mast atop the North Tower of the World Trade Center, installed in 1978.

North Tower and its 110-m (360-ft) radio mast, installed in 1978, had succumbed to the damage inflicted by American Airlines Flight 11 and collapsed. With other transmitters in the area, such as those on the spire of the nearby Empire State Building, already overcrowded, many radio and television services in New York were forced off-air until replacement transmitters were installed in the weeks and months that followed the attacks. A 3-m-long (9 ft 10-in.) fragment of the radio and television antenna was salvaged from the WTC and now forms part of the collection within the 9/11 memorial museum.

Overleaf: The Freedom Tower, New York, topped with a 124-m (408-ft) radio antenna.

Radio will soon be returning to the World Trade Center site. The 'Freedom Tower', the largest of the replacement buildings, is topped with a steel structure that is set to become New York's main radio and

television antennae once again, although this has not been without some controversy. Critics questioned whether this 124-m-tall (408-ft) structure should be classified as an architectural 'spire', or whether it should be recognized as a functional 'antenna' and therefore omitted from the official height of the building. As insignificant and semantic as this might seem, the stakes are not inconsiderable. Not only does the Freedom Tower depend on the 'spire' to achieve its much-celebrated height of 541 m (1,776 ft – a numerical reference to the year in which the United States declared independence from Great Britain), but it requires the additional 124 m (408 ft) to steal a lead on Chicago's Willis Tower as the Western hemisphere's tallest building. When the Council on Tall Buildings and Urban Habitat announced their belief that the Freedom Tower's spire was architecturally integral to the building's design (and therefore shouldn't be considered a mast), Chicago's mayor, Rahm Emanuel, somewhat forcefully disagreed:

> I would just say to all the experts gathered in one room, if it looks like an antenna, acts like an antenna, then guess what? It is an antenna.[5]

EXTREME RADIO

Manmade radio waves reflect and rebound between the Earth's surface and the upper atmosphere and can be detected almost anywhere that human beings have seen fit to inhabit. This is no unintended accident of physics. Radio's near-omnipresence is due to the development over more than a century of a detailed knowledge of the reflective and refractive qualities of the Earth's surfaces, sub-surface geology and geophysical features; of its 'terra firma' (in various states of saturation), estuaries, open seas, hills and mountain ranges as well as the ever-changing state of the ionosphere; and also of the evolution of transmission techniques and technologies that allow these qualities and features to be either embraced or overcome by radio.

It is not, however, just radio waves that have reached into the world's most extreme latitudes and environments. After the closure in 2007 of the CHAR 105.9 FM broadcasts to the small community of Alert in the northern Canadian territory of Nunavut, the distinction of being the world's most northerly radio station shifted to either Svalbard or Greenland – depending on how one thinks of a radio 'station'. Dating originally to 1933, Isfjord Radio on the west coast of Spitsbergen is a coastal radio station that provides direct communications services to the maritime traffic and offshore facilities operating in that part of the Arctic. In Greenland, the six hundred or so people who live more than 1,200 km (745 mi.) north of the Arctic Circle in Qaanaaq (formerly known as Thule) are said to receive broadcasts from the local radio station, Qaanaaq Radiunga, on 93.5 FM. Isfjord Radio is about 1 degree more northerly than Qannaaq, but since 1999 Isfjord's radio station has been automated and the living quarters turned into tourist

Isfjord Radio (78°03′08″N13° 36′04″E) on the island of Spitsbergen in Svalbard is arguably the world's most northerly radio station.

Rádio Soberania broadcasts to the occupants of Villa Las Estrellas, one of only two civilian settlements in Antarctica.

accommodation, giving Qaanaaq a moral (if not a technical) claim to being the world's most northerly radio station.

Antarctica has a surprising number of operational radio stations. Radio Nacional Arcángel San Gabriel broadcasts to the Argentine inhabitants of Esperanza Base on 15476 kHz and 97.6 MHz; Chileans can hear Rádio Soberania on 90.5 MHz in and around the research station at Villa Las Estrellas on King George Island; and the resident Americans at McMurdo Station have a choice of three radio stations – the wonderful-sounding Ice FM (104.5 FM) and the American Forces Network (or AFN, 93.9 FM), as well as a somewhat less official broadcast reportedly available on 88.7 FM. Anywhere else and this unofficial broadcast might be classified as a 'pirate radio' transmission, but in the context of Antarctica (which is governed by the 1959 Antarctic Treaty), it exists within a curious regulatory no-man's-land. The McMurdo radio stations are said to have access to an impressive music collection of between 12,000 and 20,000 vinyl records – the musical inheritance, according to base legend, of the record collection amassed by legendary AFN DJ Adrian Cronauer during the Vietnam War. Cronauer's electrifying broadcasts were later made famous by the actor Robin Williams in the film *Good Morning, Vietnam* (1987, dir. Barry Levinson).[6]

Ever since Marconi discovered that elevating a radio transmitter into the air could increase its transmission range, radio masts have grown in height and are some of the world's tallest manmade structures. The 646-m-high (2,119-ft) Radiofoniczny Ośrodek Nadawczy w Konstantynowie (Warsaw Radio Mast) was the world's tallest structure when it was built in 1974 and, even today, retains the accolade of being the second tallest structure ever built – surpassed only by the Burj Khalifa when completed in 2010. The iconic mast, which was a considerable source of Polish national pride, suffered a somewhat ignominious end in August 1991 when procedural failings during routine maintenance on the supporting guy cables led to the mast's spectacular collapse. It also brought about a temporary end to the international broadcasts of Radio Warsaw and the subsequent imprisonment of the mast's chief maintenance engineer. Despite initial optimism, the Warsaw radio mast was never rebuilt, although it continues to provoke excitement – albeit of conspiracy theorists who speculate about the role of the internally collapsing Soviet Union in the mast's downfall.

Today, the tallest structures in North America, Europe, Africa, Australia and Oceania are all radio transmitter masts or towers – the KVLY-TV mast (628.8 m/2,063 ft) in North Dakota; the Ostankino Tower (540.1 m/1,772 ft) in Moscow; the Nador transmitter (380 m/1,247 ft) in Morocco; the Naval Communication Station Harold E. Holt (387 m/ 1,270 ft) in Western Australia; and, finally, the Lualualei VLF transmitter (458 m/1,503 ft) on Oahu in Hawaii. None of these, though, come close to being the highest radio station in the world, which can be found at the extraordinary altitude of 3,597 m (11,800 ft) above sea level, near Leh in the strategically sensitive Ladakh region of northern India. The Leh station is just one part of India's national public radio broadcaster, All India Radio (AIR), which also holds the distinction of being the world's most extensive radio network, incorporating 420 individual stations and broadcasting in 23 languages and 146 regional dialects.

If the highest radio broadcasts can be traced to the northern Indian Himalayas, then the lowest can be found in Canada. The deepest live radio broadcast is attributed to Dan Lessard of the Canadian Broadcasting Cooperation (CBC), who hosted a range of interviews and live music from an emergency refuge station 2,340 m (7,677 ft) below ground level within the Creighton mine in Ontario, Canada, in 2015. While this was undertaken purely for the acquisition of a Guinness world record and used telephone cables to communicate the show to the surface for transmission, this example draws attention to a part of our planet that seems to resist radio more forcibly – the earth itself. Radio's potential as an underground safety device in mines has long been the source of technological speculation, and it was reported as early as the 1920s that experimental broadcasts had been successfully attempted in the Blue John cavern in Derbyshire, UK, at depths of 85 m (280 ft).[7] Today, the successor technology to these early experiments is called Through-the-Earth (TTE) signalling, which uses ultra-low frequencies to penetrate over 90 m (300 ft) or so into the Earth's geologic strata.

Seawater provides an equally challenging medium for effective radio communications. Unlike rock and earth, which absorb the energy of radio waves and hasten their attenuation, seawater is a highly efficient electrical conductor and causes radio waves to scatter and dissipate. As a result, most manmade radio waves barely penetrate more than a few centimetres below the surface of the sea. This proved to be a particular challenge for communications with submarines, and particularly nuclear submarines designed to remain submerged for months at a time in order to evade surface detection. One solution to this conundrum involved the Cold War investigation of ELF – 'Extremely Low Frequency' – radio waves. These waves oscillate at between 3 and 30 Hz (that is, 3–30 oscillations per second), are possessed of colossally long wavelengths of between 100,000 and 10,000 km (62,137 and 6,214 mi.), and are capable of penetrating seawater to a depth of several hundred metres. But ELF is no straightforward solution to the challenge of communicating wirelessly underwater. Building a transmitter station capable of generating waves of such vast wavelength was, and remains, a significant engineering challenge – requiring carefully chosen sites with low electrical conductivity, the generation of tremendous amounts of electrical power and vast antenna arrays capable of exploiting the Earth itself as an antenna. To date, only the U.S., Russia and India are known to have successfully constructed ELF communication facilities. The U.S. system, codenamed Project ELF, was located within heavily forested areas of Wisconsin and neighbouring Michigan between 1981 and 1982. While the trees provided useful protection from prying eyes, the sites were really selected because of the distinct sub-surface qualities provided by

The Ostankino Tower in Moscow, constructed 1966–7, is the tallest free-standing structure in Europe.

a vast underlying swathe of igneous and metamorphic rock, notable for its low electrical conductivity, known as the Laurentian/Canadian Shield geological formation. Two intersecting transmitter arrays with a combined antenna length of some 135 km (84 mi.) and requiring 2.6 megawatts of power were capable of sending messages to fully sub-merged submarines over half the surface of the Earth. Communication was, however, painfully slow. Due to the ultra-low frequency of radio waves generated (76 HZ) and the limited data that the signal could carry, it took approximately fifteen minutes to transmit one three-letter code to the U.S. submarine fleet. After a decade-long protest from anti-nuclear campaigners concerned about potential environmental effects, the U.S. navy mothballed their ELF facilities in 2004, although ELF stations in Russia (located on the Kola Peninsula near Murmansk) and India (located within the INS Kattabomman naval base in Tamil Nadu) remain operational to this day.[8] Visitors to Glen Garry forest in Scotland can still see remnants of the UK's own attempt to build an ELF station for the Royal Navy, although the project was abandoned in 1991 with little explanation after ten years of exploratory work.[9]

RADIO'S INNER WORLDS

If radio waves have their origins in highly technological surroundings, often high above the ground atop transmitter masts, they are received by listeners in rather more domestic circumstances – most often in the home, in the car or on the street, relayed through a multiplicity of different sorts of radio receivers attached to loudspeakers or head-phones. This is the 'domestic' end of radio, but it is here, in its inter-action with listeners, that radio is heard, negotiated, interpreted and given its distinctly personal meanings – meanings which are them-selves productive of what the media scholar Paddy Scannell calls highly individual 'radio worlds'.[10]

The transistor revolution and the wider availability of cheap radio receivers from the 1960s onwards transformed the radio medium in the

People listen for
news of President
Kennedy outside
a radio shop in
New York City,
22 November 1963.

contexts of both the developed and 'developing' worlds. The portability
of new radio technologies ensured that it would be open to new kinds
of mobilities, through radio's incorporation into battery-powered (and
wind-up) receivers and into the vast majority of motor vehicles produced
around the world. Internet streaming of radio has further international-
ized the transmission and reception patterns of radio programming. And
yet radio's ubiquity in the Global North can be viewed alongside regional
and local scarcity in much of the developing world where topography

British inventor
Trevor Bayliss
(1937–2018)
invented the
world's first
clockwork radio.

had made – and continues to make – radio broadcasting technically or economically challenging; where political suppression restricts access to radio through the prohibition of receiver equipment or the jamming of external broadcasts; where poverty limits the ownership of, or access to, even the most basic radio equipment; or where, held in captivity, individuals or groups of individuals are able only to hear intermittent reports from makeshift wireless tuners. For people in such situations, listening to the radio is far from mundane and everyday: it is often dangerous, frustrating and unreliable and yet, when it is heard, radio is cherished as a source of information and entertainment throughout periods of conflict, famine and political change, and as a source of companionship and support during stretches in isolation. Drawing on the mental diary he kept while a hostage in Beirut from 1987 to 1991, the Anglican Church envoy Terry Waite (b. 1939) later recalled:

> I am now one of [the BBC World Service's] most grateful listeners. I am terrified that when the batteries in my radio run out, the guards will not replace them. I cling to this little radio set obsessively. To lose it now would be terrible torture.[11]

As David Hendy notes, radio is perhaps the 'most adaptable' medium at locating its audience, even where those audiences stretch across international frontiers:

> We are . . . defined at different times and simultaneously by our membership of a nation-state, a local community, an ethnic group and a set of musical tastes. Radio almost, but not quite entirely, matches this range. While being the local medium par excellence, radio is also able to reach across large spaces, potentially threatening place-specific cultures with its homogenized content, potentially forging new delocalised communities of interest; it has a history in which nation states often led the way in establishing services, but its oral code of communication allows it to tie itself to communities of language which ignore official borders; it betrays a commercial imperative to reach large, high spending audiences, but it also has a cost structure which creates at least the possibility of a community station surviving on the tiniest of audiences.[12]

For these and other reasons, radio is often celebrated for its inclusivity, sociability and intimacy – features of radio that are also fostered through the deployment of particular programming formats, such as talk radio, which encourages an increased familiarity with the community of listeners with whom we co-inhabit our shared radio worlds.

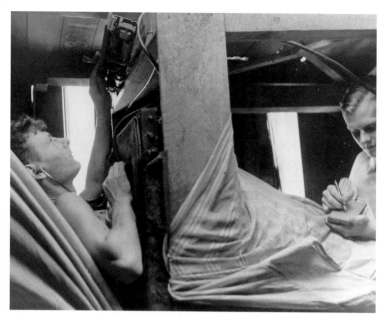

Listening in captivity:
prisoners of war
with a secret wireless
hidden in the bed
support.

Our experience of the radio world is, of course, shaped by the ways in which we, as listeners, interact and correspond with radio as a sonic/aural medium, but also as a medium that makes no straightforward appeal to our sense of sight. Given that human perception of space is considered to be intimately connected with the act of seeing, of visualizing, and with the human eye privileged as the primary sensory organ, there are questions to be asked about the effect this has on our relationship with a medium that some consider to be 'blind'. The media scholar Andrew Crissell notes:

> What strikes everyone, broadcasters and listeners alike, as significant about radio is that it is a blind medium. We cannot see its messages, they consist only of noise and silence, and it is from the sole fact of its blindness that all radio's other distinctive qualities – the nature of its language, its jokes, the way in which its audiences use it – ultimately derive.[13]

Inherent in Crissell's claims is a palpable sense that radio is, somehow, an incomplete medium, blind and less satisfactory than the combined sounds and pictures generated by, for example, television or film. Rather than being 'struck' and confronted by this loss, radio perhaps offers an alternative to the visually demanding nature of television and film and could even be considered constructive of a certain kind of alternative 'visuality' composed from listeners' experiences and memories – the 'mind's eye'.

Rejecting the 'deficiency of sound' approach to radio, the media theorist and scholar Alan Beck conceptualizes radio messages as productive of two spatializing and visually attuned concepts. First, the 'extra-radio world'. This is the world that is assembled at the point of transmissions through the interaction of radio apparatus – including

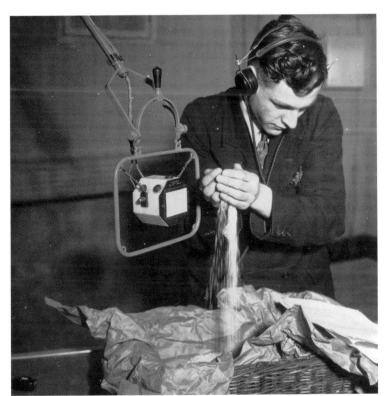

A BBC sound effects artist uses salt and brown paper to reproduce the sound of rain (1933).

the recording microphone, sound equalizers, transmitters and the radio receiver – and which is represented to listeners through the process of broadcast and reception. The second is radio's *mise en scène*, or stage-craft – composed of the locations, spaces and perspectives invoked in radio's 'sound pictures' and animated by radio's 'performers'. This goes beyond the 'sound scenery' (slamming doors or farmyard noises) essential to radio dramas and hints at a more inclusive understanding of radio's sound-spaces that responds to, and is co-constituted with, 'listener space' and what Beck refers to as radio's 'fictional time-space'.[14] Radio might thus be understood through social, mediated and fictional spaces and a powerful appeal to the imagination. In her account of 'exploratory radio listening' in the U.S. during the 1920s, the media historian and cultural critic Susan Douglas gets at this uncanny relationship between sound and space. Interwar radio provided audiences with 'out-of-body' experiences. With the turn of the radio dial (which some listeners invested with a sense of 'magic') pioneering listeners were empowered to move, electromagnetically, through a new world of local, national and international radio signals. As one 1920s pioneer observed of their nightly radio exploration: 'I can travel over the United States and yet remain at home.'

RADIO'S OTHER WORLDS

Radio waves aren't the sole preserve of humankind – and the radio spectrum is certainly not in the complete control of international regulators and national governments. Radio remains a natural physical phenomenon – and radio waves are the product of natural sources as well as artificial ones. As we turn the tuning dial on a traditional analogue radio receiver, the strong signals of familiar radio stations are interspersed with the distinctive hiss of what we often call 'white noise' or 'static'. In these spaces, the background noise is an expression of naturally occurring radio waves that come from a variety of earthly and other-worldly sources. During thunderstorms, for example, the discharge of electromagnetic energy that appears to us as a visible flash of lightning also produces invisible pulses of radio waves that discharge through the upper atmosphere. These pulses can be heard on radio receivers up to several thousand kilometres from the original lightning strike and are known as 'sferics' (short for 'atmospherics') – distinctive 'tweeks' or 'whistlers' depending on the distance of travel and whether the signals have entered the Earth's 'magnetosphere'. The British progressive rock band Pink Floyd incorporated more than a minute's worth of these atmospheric ticks in an extended instrumental section at the start of the *Division Bell* album from 1994. The tweeks and whistlers were apparently recorded at the top of Mount Washington in the U.S. state of Vermont, but caused confusion among even the most dedicated fans of the British band, who thought the noises were the result of a manufacturing error rather than the band's attempt to share 'space noise'.

While Pink Floyd's 'space noise' had distinctly earthly origins, the forces that created the universe continue to rebound within and beyond our atmosphere and do so in the form of radio waves between 1–30GHz (predominantly), known as 'cosmic microwave background

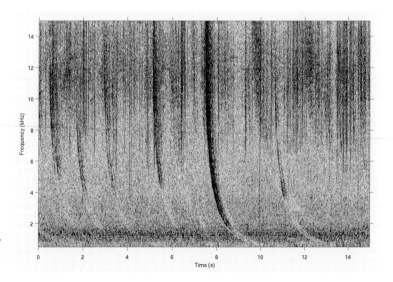

'Whistlers' and other
sferics, recorded on a
VLF receiver.

radiation' (CMBR). The accidental discovery of this 'relic radiation' was as controversial as it was sensational when it was announced in 1964 – providing, as it did, the most compelling evidence yet to substantiate the Big Bang theory for the creation of the universe. The two American physicists responsible for the discovery, Arno Penzias and Robert Wilson, were experimenting with early satellite communications for Bell Telephone Laboratories in Holmdel, New Jersey, using a 6-m (19-ft-8-in.) 'horn antenna' to detect radio waves reflected off 'echo balloon' satellites. To measure the faint traces of these radio waves, all recognizable interference had to be eradicated from the receiver. The effects of radar and radio broadcasting were removed, and interference produced by heat within the receiver was suppressed by cooling it with liquid helium to −269°C (−452°F), only 4 kelvin above absolute zero.

The horn reflector antenna, built 1959, at Bell Telephone Laboratories in Holmdel, New Jersey.

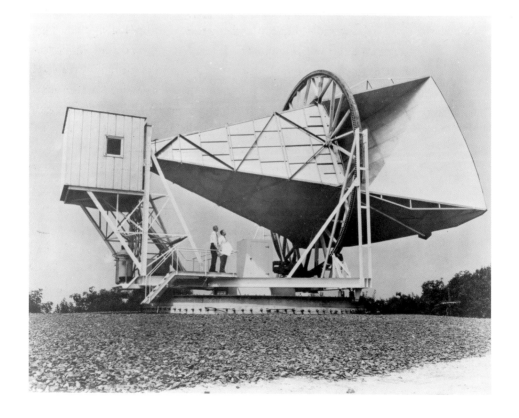

Notwithstanding these efforts, a mysterious noise with a 7.35-cm (2.89-in.) wavelength persisted in the receiver; one that was one hundred times stronger than anticipated, spread evenly across the sky and present day and night. After further eliminating the possibility that the equipment was being affected by nesting pigeons and their accumulated droppings (by literally eliminating the pigeons), the scientists came to realize that the noise was both *real* and originated from *outside* our own galaxy. In their quest to produce commercial satellite communications, the two men had inadvertently discovered the remnants of the high-energy radiation released at the moment of the Big Bang – the flash of searing light which, after 13.798 billion years of cosmic expansion and cooling, had been stretched and diminished of energy to the point that they could be 'heard' as radio waves. Penzias and Wilson won the Nobel Prize for their discovery in 1978.

Today, radio telescopes, the successor technologies to the 'horn antenna', continually monitor the skies listening for cosmic activity, not all of which is the remnant of the ancient light of the Big Bang. As well as visible light, stars (including our own sun) and galaxies produce radio waves, while other astronomical objects undetectable by optical astronomy, including 'radio-loud' pulsars, quasars and 'radio galaxies', have only been discovered thanks to the advances of radio astronomy since the 1930s. Karl Jansky, another employee of Bell Telephone Laboratories at their Holmdel site, is considered to be the father of radio astronomy following his chance discovery of radio waves emanating from the centre of the Milky Way in 1931. Modern radio telescopes are somewhat larger and more powerful than Jansky's original. Dubbed 'Jansky's merry-go-round', it had a diameter of approximately 30 m (98 ft 5 in.), stood 6 m (19 ft 8 in.) tall, and could pinpoint a radio signal by physically rotating on a set of four tyres sourced from a Model-T Ford.

Radio telescopes are some of the largest and most costly pieces of scientific equipment ever produced, and their immense scale has ensured that many of these telescopes have become firmly lodged in the popular lexicon of twentieth-century science. The 76.2-m-diameter

(250-ft) Lovell Telescope at Jodrell Bank in the UK has featured in novels, films, television programmes, music videos and on the stamps of at least seven different countries since it was commissioned in 1957. The 64-m (210-ft) Parkes radio telescope is located, somewhat modestly, in the middle of a sheep paddock in rural New South Wales in Australia but shot to international attention when it relayed the television pictures of Neil Armstrong's moonwalk in July 1969, and then again when the film *The Dish* (2000, dir. Rob Sitch) retold the story of Parkes's role

The Jodrell Bank radio telescope (opened in 1957), renamed the Lovell Telescope in 1987.

in the Apollo 11 mission for a new generation. At 305 m (1,000 ft) in diameter, the Arecibo Observatory in Puerto Rico is the world's second largest 'single aperture' radio telescope and the backdrop for the denouement of the 1995 James Bond movie *GoldenEye* (dir. Martin Campbell). Arecibo, which had been the world's largest single aperture telescope for 53 years, was overtaken in 2016 by the 'Five-hundred-metre Aperture Spherical Telescope' (FAST) – otherwise known as the Eye of Heaven – nestled into the hilltops of Guizhou Province in China. The world's most powerful radio telescopes are, in fact, arrays of closely coordinated radio telescopes that work together to enhance their power and field of vision. Some notable examples include the 27 individual dishes that make up the Karl G. Jansky Very Large Array (VLA) in New Mexico, the thirty wire dishes of the Giant Metrewave Radio Telescope (GMRT) in Pune, India, and the Chinese Spectral Radio Heliograph (CSRH), which will be formed of one hundred telescopes, and is

The Parkes radio observatory, New South Wales, Australia.

currently under construction in Inner Mongolia. There are currently plans for a 'Square Kilometre Array' to be built in South Africa and Australia, with its headquarters at Jodrell Bank, which will, when completed, have a total collecting area of 1 sq. km (over ⅓ sq. mi.) and will be the world's most sensitive and expensive radio instrument.

It is worthwhile noting that radio telescopes, although designed to be highly attuned receivers of cosmic radio waves, can also become extremely effective transmitters if the occasion requires. One such occasion came in 1974 following the completion of renovations to the Arecibo radio telescope in Puerto Rico. To mark the occasion, an interstellar radio message carrying basic information about the planet Earth, human beings and human genetics was transmitted in the direction of a globular star cluster, known as M13, in the hope that intelligent extraterrestrial life might receive and decipher it. The 1974 'Arecibo Message', written in binary digits and laced with prime numbers and other mathematical references, will take nearly 25,000 years to reach M13 and, presumably, at least another 25,000 years for a response to be received on Earth. Carl Sagan, the popular American astronomer and science communicator, was one of this message's

The Arecibo Message, an interstellar radio communication carrying basic information about humanity and Earth, was sent to globular star cluster M13 in 1974.

The Arecibo Observatory's radio telescope, Puerto Rico.

authors. In a curious blurring of science fact and science fiction, Sagan's subsequent novel, *Contact* (1985), tells the story of a promising astronomer and radio hobbyist who detects an incoming radio message of extraterrestrial origins – composed, just as the genuine 1974 message, in binary and laced with mathematical referents. The film version of the book (1997, dir. Robert Zemeckis), starring Jodie Foster, was filmed at both the Arecibo telescope and New Mexico's Jansky VLA.

2

MAKING WAVES

On 4 August 1898, in the twilight years of her reign, Queen Victoria, empress of India, was elevated into a new state of ascendency. After 79 years rooted to the Earth's surfaces of earth and water, Queen Victoria took to the air and ushered into being a new era of royal communications. This was no physical disconnection from the Earth, however. From the parlour of Ladywood Cottage, within the grounds of Osborne House on the Isle of Wight, the Queen dictated a brief message to her son Edward, the Prince of Wales, who was convalescing on board the royal yacht in the Solent. Forgoing the traditional services of a royal messenger (who would deliver the note on foot) or horseback courier, the Queen's good wishes were translated into Morse code, tapped out on a telegrapher's key and transmitted into and through the air before, almost instantaneously, being detected on a similar receiving system installed on HMY *Osborne*. Over the course of the following week, a further 150 wireless messages passed between the royal yacht and the Queen's household. The Queen was reported to be personally 'delighted' with the new technology even if the presence of a new breed of electronic engineer somewhat unsettled the strictly observed protocols of Osborne House. The provider of this new means of wireless communication was the 25-year-old Italian upstart Guglielmo Marconi, who, within less than three years of arriving in England, had risen to become one of the most celebrated entrepreneurs in the country.

The early history of radio is mired in controversy, accusations of intellectual theft and dishonesty, patent infringements, disputed court rulings, spurious science, enormous egos, self-publicity and disputed legacies. It is a history animated by the basest of human instincts, ambition and greed, but also by undisputed genius and the triumph of the human imagination. While this story recalls some of the most eminent names in science during the late nineteenth and early twentieth centuries, including James Clerk Maxwell, Heinrich Rudolf Hertz and Guglielmo Marconi, it has also failed to remember – even silenced – the contributions made by rather less well-known names such as Reginald Fessenden, Oliver Lodge, Jagadish Chandra Bose and Nikola Tesla, as well as dozens of others besides. It is a narrative – or perhaps more accurately, a whole series of parallel and interlocking scientific genealogies – that continues to arouse passionate and somewhat nationalistic arguments from academic scholars and radio enthusiasts

HMY *Osborne* passing through the Kiel Canal, 1895.

in support or censure of the key actors and their behaviours, their achievements and their limitations. For much of the twentieth century, these stories appear to have been told with the express purpose of addressing an important yet thorny question. 'Who invented radio?'

Guglielmo Marconi (1874–1937), wireless pioneer.

The elusiveness of a straightforward answer to this question, and the challenge of attributing primacy of invention, is largely related to our naive use of the word 'radio' as though it were a singular technology. The reality is actually quite different. The radio sets that we find in our homes and cars, and which can today be picked up for about the price of a cup of coffee, are the product of an extraordinary history of incremental invention, experimentation and discovery – driven by an international cast of scientists, inventors, engineers and entrepreneurs who, during the one hundred years from 1820 to 1920, transformed the world. This may seem like a rather grandiose overstatement and a descent into hyperbole, but if it does it is only because the revolutions in human communication achieved during that century of progress continue to be so poorly understood. In 1820 information could only be transmitted from person to person at the speed at which human beings could travel – on foot, or conveyed by coach, ship or on horseback. When the announcement of the birth of Princess Alexandrina Victoria (later Queen Victoria) was posted outside Kensington Palace in 1819, the news would have taken about sixteen hours to reach the postmaster in the city of Bristol by mail coach, and fifty hours to reach Edinburgh. By the time Queen Victoria died in 1901, the electric telegraph carried the announcement within seconds to telegraph stations throughout the United Kingdom and, via a global network of submarine cables, to the British Empire and around the world. The thin red lines inked onto maps from commercial companies such the Eastern Telegraph Company represented nothing short of a Victorian communications revolution – the material trace of what Tom Standage would later describe as the 'Victorian Internet'.[1] The sociologist Lewis Mumford would describe the electric telegraph in even more prosaic terms: the latest in a series of 'space-annihilating devices, by means of which man was enabled to express himself at a distance'.[2] And not just man. Woman too. Queen Victoria herself, in fact. Freed of earthly webs of wire and insulation, experiments in wireless telegraphy of the 1890s seemed not only to promise the *annihilation* of distance and the *conquest* of space, but dominion in the skies and in the ether. Within the eighteen months that followed her death, Queen Victoria's favoured 'electrician' would push the bounds of wireless telegraphy still further, traversing the Atlantic and wirelessly linking the British Isles with the Dominion of Canada for the first time.

Guglielmo Marconi was born in Bologna in 1874 into a wealthy Italian-Irish family. His mother, Annie, was from the famed Jameson family of whisky distillers, and this status provided the young Marconi with the opportunity to read widely – his youthful reading list included works by eminent European physicists such as Oliver Lodge and Heinrich Hertz – and also to forge a career in experimental science that started while he was still in his late teens. Marconi was fascinated by electricity and set about creating devices that could both detect its natural occurrence in the form of lightning strikes and, separately, harness electromagnetic radiation as a means of communication. This was no solitary endeavour, and even as a very young man Marconi was effective in marshalling much-needed assistance in his experimental enterprises. On the occasion in September 1895 when Marconi successfully transmitted a wireless signal over a distance of 2 km (1¼ mi.), for example, he was ably assisted by the family butler and various estate workers from the family's palatial Villa Griffone. Marconi left Italy only a short time later, arriving in England in 1896 with the hope of securing intellectual and financial support for his experimental apparatus. Still only 22 years old, Marconi proved to be a gifted operator. He deftly navigated entry into the more cerebral quarters of London society, while his concepts enjoyed growing support from influential sections of the scientific community. It is telling that within only two years of Marconi's arrival in London he was replicating the Griffone transmissions at the heart of the British imperial metropole, relaying messages back and forth across the River Thames from the Houses of Parliament to St Thomas' Hospital. On this occasion assistance was not supplied by the Marconi family butler but, instead, by William Court Gully, the Speaker of the House of Commons.

Marconi's acceptance into British scientific and establishment society was rapid, even if it wasn't a complete adoption. When, for example, Marconi was invited to Osborne House to demonstrate his technology to Queen Victoria's Royal Household, he committed the extraordinary faux pas of strolling across the Queen's private lawns, an offence that saw him rather unceremoniously ejected from the estate.[3] 'Get another electrician,' the Queen is reported to have announced; only to be informed by an attendant: 'Alas, your Majesty, England has no Marconi.' The young Italian inventor was quickly retrieved from his hotel and brought back to Osborne, where he was granted an audience with the Queen. 'She was seventy-nine years old, he was barely out of boyhood,' notes Erik Larsen, 'but he spoke with the confidence of a Lord Salisbury, and she was charmed.'[4] The messages that bounced back and forth between Osborne House and the royal yacht provide a lasting insight into the working of the British Royal Family in the late Victorian period, but just as importantly are revealing of an extraordinary, albeit brief, collision of scientific enquiry, public relations and the mystique of royalty. Masterfully engineered by the young Marconi, this encounter was as much a product of genuine scientific experimentation as it was an expression of an emerging mythology around radio and those who sought to harness its capacities.

Radio's emergence as a global communications phenomenon didn't simply require the skilled showmanship of Marconi. To make radio work in anything like its modern form, electricity's role in communications had first to be established; radio waves needed to be artificially produced, reliably detected over distance, and their frequencies manipulated; sounds – whether voices or music – needed to be captured and radiated through the air; and ultimately systems and devices for distribution and reception were required. The communications revolution that produced these developments was a distinctly slow kind of affair. Somewhat introverted. Quiet, ironically. Particularly by comparison with the noise, the energy and the bombast of the scientists, inventors and entrepreneurs of the heavy industries that had dramatically altered the physical and social landscape of Britain, Europe and the United States during the mid- to late nineteenth century. And yet, without the intricate investigations of scientists working soberly in laboratories in the field of electromagnetics, many of what we consider to be the great achievements of the 'technological revolution' – what Vaclav Smil would call the 'age of synergy' – might never have come to pass, nor had their potential fully realized.[5] The harnessing of electromagnetism for the purposes of communication allowed not only for the sharing of scientific ideas, but for the connection and coordination of machinery and whole factories into something that resembled an industrial infrastructure – a system of production and distribution, supply and demand that could be made efficient and profitable through communication and close synchronization.

CABLES AND WIRELESS

During a mid-lecture demonstration of electricity at the University of Copenhagen in April 1820, Professor Hans Christian Ørsted (1777–1851) made an unexpected discovery. Quite by chance, he observed that a compass needle ever-so-slightly twitched when in close proximity to a wire carrying a modest electrical current, momentarily deflecting from magnetic north. 'The effect was', as Ørsted later acknowledged, 'very feeble', and the demonstration 'made no strong impression on the audience', and yet Ørsted had – albeit unintentionally – demonstrated that magnetism and electricity were closely linked phenomena.[6] Within little more than a year, the English scientist Michael Faraday (1791–1867) had built on Ørsted's observation and demonstrated a 'homopolar motor' at the Royal Institution in London. While of little practical value, Faraday's motor – essentially a piece of loose-hanging wire dipped in a mercury pool in which a magnet was placed – demonstrated that magnets and current-carrying wires produced rotational force. Another decade later and Faraday's research into electromagnetic induction demonstrated that a changing magnetic field could induce electric currents at a distance.

Within little more than a decade following Ørsted's chance observation, it was already possible for scientists and engineers to contemplate the scientific potential for 'transmitting' messages over considerable distances using electromagnetism. Within another five years, even these contemplations had given way to fully practicable systems for communicating by wire when, in 1837, William Cooke (1806–1879) and Charles Wheatstone (1802–1875) demonstrated their electric telegraph. Seeing the potential of telegraph to improve the safety of Britain's new railways, Cooke and Wheatstone collaborated with the famed engineer Isambard Kingdom Brunel (1806–1859) to link stations along the Great Western Railway, beginning with a 21-km (13-mi.) section between Paddington Station and West Drayton (opened in July 1839). By 1843, Slough was also connected. From here, the Cooke and

Michael Faraday
demonstrating
a homopolar
motor at the Royal
Institution, London,
1846.

PROFESSOR FARADAY'S LECTURE AT THE ROYAL INSTITUTION.

Wheatstone system spread across the country and, by the turn of the twentieth century, some 15,000 telegraphs were in operation across Britain's railway network, the last only being decommissioned in the 1930s. The Cooke and Wheatstone business relationship didn't endure quite so long. After years of growing acrimony and arbitration, Cooke, the go-getting entrepreneur, and Wheatstone, the King's College professor of Physics, parted company in 1845.

As with almost all stories in the history and development of radio, the primacy of Cooke and Wheatstone's achievements are open to debate and international dispute, thanks largely to the mobility of ideas in post-Enlightenment Europe. Pavel Schilling (1786–1837), a Russian scientist and diplomat, built an electromagnetic telegraph as early as 1828, which he demonstrated in 1832 by transmitting a message between two rooms of his apartment in St Petersburg. The Russian Admiralty

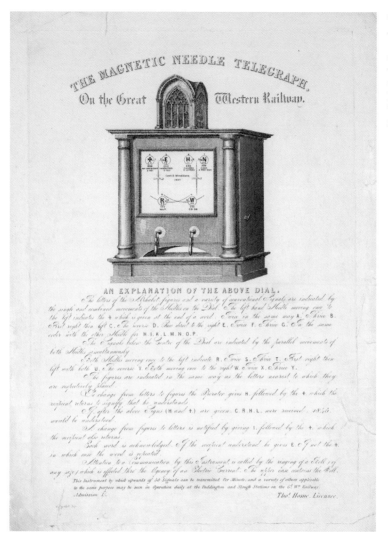

G. Bartlett, *The Magnetic Needle Telegraph*, c. 1843, engraving. The device was first used on the Great Western Railway between West Drayton and Slough.

subsequently tested his technology over a distance of 5 km (3 mi.) via a cable that was routed between buildings, across roads and through the waters of a canal. Schilling's telegraph was also demonstrated at the university in Heidelberg. William Cooke, freshly discharged from the British-Indian army, was inspired to make telegraphy his life's work after attending one such demonstration in 1836.[7] Back in England, the meteorologist and inventor Francis Ronalds (1788–1873) is credited with constructing a rudimentary telegraph at his home in Hammersmith, west London, as early as 1816. Using his back garden as an outdoor laboratory, he demonstrated that messages could be sent, via wire, over a range of about 150 m (492 ft). The designs were never patented, and one gets a sense from Ronalds's writings that national defence was a greater priority than the prospect of financial reward. As Schilling would do a decade or so later in Russia, Ronalds offered his technology to the British Admiralty, believing that it might substantially improve communications between London and Portsmouth (which, at the time, relied on a chain of fifteen optical semaphore stations), only to have his offer rejected by John Barrow, the Admiralty's secretary.[8] Undeterred, Ronalds described his invention and its possible applications in a small pamphlet published in 1823:

> Why should not our government govern at Portsmouth almost as promptly as in Downing Street? Why should our defaulters escape by default of our foggy climate? . . . Let us have *electrical conversazione offices* communicating with each other all over the kingdom, *if we can.*[9]

Unlike Schilling, who died in 1837, Ronalds lived long enough to see his prophecies fulfilled and then overtaken by the telegraph's international expansion across the Atlantic. Ronalds was finally recognized for his 'early and remarkable labours in telegraphic investigations' with the award of a knighthood in 1870, three years before he died. The Soviet Union recognized Schilling's contribution in 1982, the 150th anniversary of the demonstration of his telegraph system, when they placed his image on perhaps the most enduring of communications technologies, a stamp.

By the 1860s, James Clerk Maxwell had witnessed and been impressed by the success of the telegraph but was also aware of some of the difficulties that telegraphers faced and endured. Electromagnetic distortion – 'retardation' – severely affected long-range communication over wires, particularly in submarine environments. While William Thomson (1824–1907, later to become Lord Kelvin) would ultimately find a practicable solution to these challenges during the laying of the second Atlantic cable in 1866 (the first having failed due to degradation caused by excessive voltages), James Clerk Maxwell sought a rigorous theoretical solution. In undertaking this pursuit, Maxwell went on to produce a coherent theory – expressed through a series of mathematical equations – on electric and magnetic effects and their mutual interaction. These formulae revealed two enormously significant breakthroughs for modern science. First, he demonstrated that electromagnetic energy does not travel in a straight unwavering line, preferring instead to oscillate in the form a wave; and that, secondly, these waves of electromagnetic energy travel at a speed almost identical to that of the known speed of light. For Maxwell, this similarity was more than a coincidence. Writing in 1864, he noted:

Pavel Schilling, telegraph pioneer, as commemorated on a Soviet stamp, 1982.

> The agreement of the results seems to show that light and magnetism are affections of the same substance, and that light is an electromagnetic disturbance propagated through the field according to electromagnetic laws.[10]

The theoretical physics that underpinned Maxwell's thesis confounded the scientific establishment. Physicists struggled to grasp the complex mathematics while mathematicians struggled to comprehend the physical concepts being proposed. And yet, Maxwell's scientific achievement was revolutionary. By recognizing that light and magnetism were two expressions of the same force, he conjoined the science of electromagnetics and the science of light into one expanded understanding of electromagnetism. Just as Sir Isaac Newton produced the first 'unification in physics' by conjoining the sciences of physics and astronomy, so Maxwell had produced the 'second great unification'.[11] In doing so, Maxwell laid the foundations for the subsequent development of all wireless communications – even if Maxwell's waves remained locked in the abstract world of mathematical theory during his lifetime.

It would be another twenty years before the German physicist Heinrich Hertz (1857–1894) was able to develop the apparatus required to fully realize Maxwell's theory. Using a 'spark gap' connected to a piece of wire 1 metre (3¼ ft) long as a means of creating electromagnetic radiation and a basic antenna set some distance away, Hertz produced, detected and conclusively demonstrated the existence of

Kimmel & Forster, 'The Eighth Wonder of the World – the Atlantic Cable', 1865, colour lithograph.

THE EIGHTH WONDER OF THE WORLD.
THE ATLANTIC CABLE.

Hertz's sketch of
electromagnetic
waves produced by
a 'spark gap', 1888.

electromagnetic waves. Soon after, using parabolic reflectors, Hertz was also able to demonstrate that radio waves (widely known as 'Hertzian waves' until around 1910) could be reflected and focused just like visible light. In 1960 the General Conference on Weights and Measures, the body which administers the International System of Units (SI), recognized Hertz's contribution to the science of electromagnetism when the standard measure of frequency, previously 'cycles per second', was renamed 'hertz' (HZ) in his honour.

As with many who had come before them both Maxwell and Hertz were pure scientists who neither recognized nor wished to contemplate the practical applications of their discoveries. Reflecting on the significance of his particular work on electromagnetism, Hertz is reputed to have declared to his students at the University of Bonn:

It is no use whatsoever . . . this is just an experiment that proves Maestro Maxwell was right. We just have these mysterious electromagnetic waves that we cannot see with the naked eye. But they are there.[12]

One student is said to have responded, 'So, what's next?' The answer, which one can imagine being delivered with shrugged shoulders and a redundant sigh was, 'Nothing, I guess'. The reality would, of course, be rather different. Hertz's English counterpart in mathematical physics, Sir Oliver Heaviside (1850–1925), perhaps had it right in 1891. 'Three years ago electromagnetic waves were nowhere,' he observed. 'Shortly afterward, they were everywhere.'[13]

RADIO SPECTACULAR

By the turn of the twentieth century, the quiet science of electromagnetism had become uproarious theatre. Public demonstrations of electricity 'jumping' through the air and of 'magical' wireless signals working over considerable distances enthralled, entertained and mystified audiences in equal measure. Advertisements for the inaugural 'Electrical Exhibition' held in New York's Madison Square Garden in May 1898 invited visitors to witness the 'moving marvels' of the electrical age, the 'spectacle' of 'Engines, Dynamos, Pumps, Printing Plants'. If that all seemed rather too masculine, the promoters also highlighted the 'Electrical Cradle, Electrical Cooking, Electrical Flatiron . . . Electrical Five o'Clock Teas – no wonder the women are interested'.[14]

Nikola Tesla, the Serbian-American inventor who had already achieved notoriety by harnessing Alternating Current (AC) as a means of distributing electricity, used the occasion of the show to give a special viewing of his latest project to a group of friends and potential investors, including George Westinghouse (1846–1914), J. P. Morgan (1837–1913) and W. K. Vanderbilt (1849–1920). At only about 1.2 m (4 ft) in length and 0.9 m (3 ft) in height, with a copper hull and domed roofline, Tesla's particular investment opportunity wasn't necessarily all that striking a proposition, but the science and technology contained within the hull and control unit of the boat floating in the purpose-built tank were years ahead of their time. As one newspaper reported of the demonstration:

Tesla's automaton, U.S. patent number 613,809 (July 1898).

> *New York, 1898.* 'Now watch,' said the inventor, and going to a table on the other side of the room, on which lay a little switch box, he gave the lever a sharp turn. Instantly the little propeller began to revolve. 'Now I will send the boat to starboard,' he added, and another movement of the lever sent the helm sharp over, and another motion turned it back again.[15]

Without wires, and without anyone seeming to influence its movement, the boat moved across the surface of the water, turned, stopped, reversed and even communicated with the onlooking audience by flashing its lights in answer to their questions – all using the power of radio waves. Reports suggest that some of the onlookers thought Tesla's invention to be a work of magic; others considered it to be an elaborate hoax, perhaps using a trained monkey contained within the boat's hull to influence its movements.

For most of the onlookers, Tesla's radio-controlled boat – a fusion of mechanical engineering and electromagnetic science – was simply beyond their late nineteenth-century comprehension. Tesla's accompanying philosophy probably didn't help dispel their confusion, or caution. Tesla proclaimed his boat to be the first of a kind of 'automaton', a new form of automated being that might even, in time, 'act as though possessed of reason and without any wilful control from the outside'.[16] If loaded with explosives, automatons in the seas and in the skies might bring about the abolition of human conflict. When even the most 'feeble' of nations are capable of accessing weaponry that would make them 'impregnable to the united armadas of the world', claimed Tesla, then war itself would become obsolete.[17]

No. 613,809.

N. TESLA.

Patented Nov. 8, 1898.

METHOD OF AND APPARATUS FOR CONTROLLING MECHANISM OF MOVING VESSELS
OR VEHICLES.

(No Model.)

5 Sheets—Sheet 3.

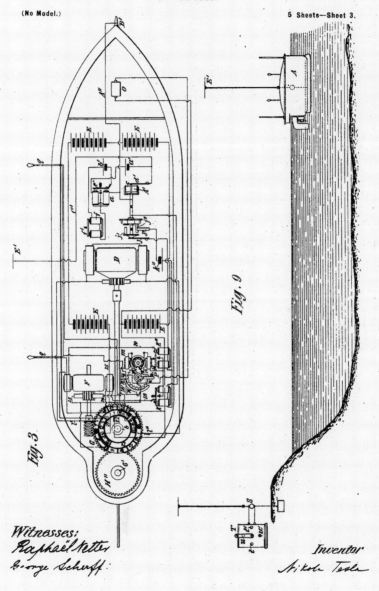

Fig. 9

Fig. 3

Witnesses:

Raphaël Netter

George Scherff

Inventor

Nikola Tesla

WONDERS NIKOLA TESLA SAYS HE CAN PERFORM.
Shows How He Proposes by Electricity, Without Wires, to Control the Movements of a Model at the Paris Exposition from His Office in New York, and by Similar Methods Blow Up Ironclads and Send Lifeboats to Shipwrecked Vessels.

Imagining a future in which 'automatons' are controlled from other continents, from the *New York Herald*, 8 November 1898.

Viewed retrospectively, we can see in Tesla's invention and philosophizing something remarkably akin to what we would now call drones. For all this prescience, though, Tesla's philosophies drew scorn and derision during his lifetime and his radio-controlled automaton appeared to sink without trace from public attention. Perhaps his ideas were too fanciful and his technologies just too futuristic for *fin-de-siècle* audiences. What is certain about the 1898 exhibition is that Tesla, a noted master of publicity and 'the spectacular', had been significantly outgunned by a rival wireless innovator with an eye for *realpolitik*. Newspaper reports from this exhibition made comparatively little mention of Tesla's boat, saving their column inches to report on an apparently even more dramatic and explosive exhibit that wirelessly detonated mines attached to the underside of model Spanish warships (the Spanish–American War having broken out in April 1898). 'The man who fires the mines in the tank and blows up the cruisers without a wire holds the Hertzian wave practically under his telegraph key,' the *New York Times* reported, 'and although some of the visitors about the tank get a little sprinkling when the water rises, it is taken good

naturedly and the time for each explosion is awaited eagerly.'[18] The man
in question was William J. Clarke, a wireless entrepreneur representing
the United States Electrical Supply Company, but the wireless technology that enabled his demonstration was attributed to the young
Anglo-Italian entrepreneur Guglielmo Marconi, whose own wireless
career was hitting even greater heights.

For Tesla, the events of 1898 established an unfortunate pattern that
would recur throughout much of the remainder of his career. Despite
his extraordinary inventiveness and creativity, his work was frequently
overlooked, misunderstood and actively disparaged in the scientific
community and in New York's circuit of well-heeled financiers. While
initially supportive of his Italian counterpart – 'Marconi is a good
fellow. Let him continue. He is using seventeen of my patents,' Tesla is
reported to have said in 1901 – Tesla become increasingly embittered
when, in 1904, the U.S. Patent Office mysteriously overturned Tesla's
patents, and awarded a patent that effectively attributed the invention of radio to Marconi.[19] He was further enraged when Marconi was
awarded the 1909 Nobel Prize for his contribution to the development
of wireless telegraphy. A series of business failures left Tesla without the
financial means of pursuing legal action against the U.S. Patent Office
through the U.S. courts. In fact, Tesla wouldn't see justice served during
his lifetime. He spent most of the rest of his life in a perilous financial
state, living in hotels and acquiring a growing string of creditors. He
died in January 1943. In June of the same year, the U.S. Supreme Court
adjudicated on several patents held by the U.S. Marconi Company and
invalidated most of them on the basis of 'prior art' – that is to say
their prior invention by earlier patent holders.[20] One of the patents
restored was U.S. Patent 645,576 for a 'System of transmission of electrical energy'. The original assignee is recorded as Nikola Tesla of New
York. In restoring Tesla's patent, the U.S. Supreme Court correspondingly restored Tesla's rightful claim to have been the one of radio's most
important inventors.

RADIO IN AND OF THE AIR

'La calma della mia vita ebbe allora fine' (The calm of my life ended then), Marconi noted to a friend when recalling the successful completion of wireless tests in May 1897. Observed by contingents of invited engineers and scientists, Marconi's system transmitted and received wireless signals over distances of 91 m, then 1.6 km, then 9.7 km and finally nearly 14.5 km (100 yards, 1 mi., 6 mi. and nearly 9 mi.) across the Bristol Channel between Lavernock Point in south Wales and Brean Down in Somerset. This was a record for wireless transmission at that time, and all the more astonishing because it had been achieved over water – a feat previously considered almost impossible. Within the weeks and months that followed, Marconi and his chief assistant George Kemp (1857–1933) built on this success and by October 1897 linked the cities of Bath and Salisbury, 55 km (34 mi.) apart, with a wireless signal. Kemp's illustrations of the experimental apparatus reveal that these gains were not simply a product of increased transmitter power or the heighted sensitivity of receivers. Height above ground – elevation – had become a determining factor. In a near inversion of Benjamin Franklin's famous experiments with lightning, Marconi used kites and even hydrogen-filled balloons to elevate his manmade generators of electromagnetism and corresponding receiving aerials more than 76 m (250 ft) above the surface of the Earth. Mastery of the air would require Marconi's apparatus to be 'in' the air.

Notoriety followed success. The British press had dubbed the young Marconi 'the inventor of wireless' following a dramatic public demonstration in London's Toynbee Hall in December 1896. Marconi's scientific contemporaries were often less generous. Professor Oliver Lodge (1851–1940), in particular, asserted his own contribution to the developing story of wireless, making it well known within scientific circles that Marconi's apparatus included a 'coherer' – a basic radio-wave detector made up of a glass tube containing metal filings that allows electrical currents to pass through when subjected to

A mobile transmitter
used in Marconi's
early wireless
experiments,
c. 1900.

electromagnetic radiation – that closely resembled those developed
by the French physicist Édouard Branly (1844–1940) during the early
1890s. Lodge had further modified Branly's design and had frequently
demonstrated its utility as a radio-wave detector over increasingly large
distances during 1894, including at the British Association for the
Advancement of Science at Oxford University. When Lodge eventually sought to patent his design in 1897, his application was rejected.

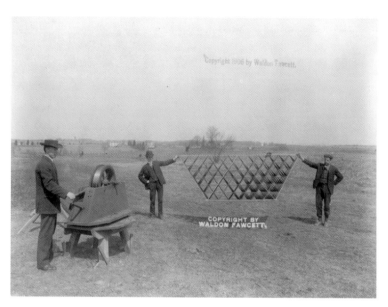

A trapezoidal
kite used in
wireless telegraphy
experiments,
c. 1906.

Marconi had got there first. Lodge would later seek to use his 1894
lecture as evidence of the primacy of his own invention of wireless
telegraphy in a dispute with the Marconi Company – although this
only exposed deeper rifts within the scientific community at the time.
The eminent physicist Silvanus P. Thompson came out in support of
Lodge, whereas the famed physicist and radio innovator J. A. Fleming
(1849–1945) suggested that Lodge's lectures were given in the spirit
of science experiments rather than as a true demonstration of wireless
telegraphy. Writing in 1899, Fleming really pinned his colours to the
mast by declaring Marconi's wireless experiments to have ushered in a
new phase of human progress: 'the Ether age'.[21]

Just as kites and balloons elevated wireless signals into the skies,
so too did they extend their horizons. In November 1897 Marconi
established the world's first permanent wireless station on the Isle of
Wight, complete with a 36.6-m-tall (120-ft) transmitter mast, and by
March 1899 had undertaken the world's first international wireless
transmission – across the English Channel, between the South Foreland lighthouse on England's south coast and the village of Wimereux

near Boulogne.[22] This was science elevated to the level of international spectacle. Marconi ensured that representatives of the French government, army and navy were present to witness the proceedings, alongside French and British newspaper reporters. The radio silence was broken by the dots and dashes of Morse code emanating from the makeshift facilities in Normandy: • • • – (meaning 'V', for Victory). The exchange of messages that followed, including telegrams of congratulations from around the United Kingdom, so impressed the French government and military observers that they offered the use of naval vessels to help Marconi undertake more detailed tests of his system. But this was not a straightforward victory. When Marconi attempted to communicate with a third wireless station on the lighthouse ship known as the East Goodwin Lightvessel, chaos ensued. The signals from the three stations interfered and effectively jammed one another – not so much because all three were transmitting on the same frequency, but because all of them were transmitting on so many frequencies. If wireless were to have

Oliver Lodge
(1851–1940) in his
laboratory in 1892.

any prospect of forming a functional network, transmitters would require to be 'tuned' so that the electromagnetic radiation they produced occupied only specific parts of the spectrum.

Oliver Lodge's work on what he called 'syntony', first patented in 1897, demonstrated that the tuning of electromagnetic waves was possible in both theory and practice. Over the following weeks, Marconi and his assistants were gradually able to reduce the spread of radiation from the various stations to the extent that South Foreland and East Goodwin could communicate 'without Wimereux receiving a single dot'.[23] Marconi, according to some sources, was careful not to breach Lodge's patent, but not untypically his work sparked controversy and rancour within and beyond the scientific establishment.[24] Oliver Lodge eventually sued Marconi for patent infringements in 1910 and settled for £15,000 and a position as a paid adviser.[25] Meanwhile, the magician, illusionist and wireless hobbyist Nevil Maskelyne, unconvinced by Marconi's claims to have created 'secure channels' for wireless communication, took up arms in an acrimonious anti-Marconi campaign. Over the following years, Maskelyne publically chided Marconi in the pages of the *Electrician* journal, but his *pièce de résistance* was saved for 1903, when he spectacularly hacked into a live demonstration of Marconi's wireless system at London's Royal Institution. As the showcase was about to begin, the wireless apparatus on stage started tapping out unexpected messages. In the first instance the word 'rats' was repeated multiple times, followed by rather more personal messages. One ditty announced: 'There was a young fellow of Italy, who diddled the public quite prettily.' Other insults followed. Maskelyne, located in a nearby theatre, had hijacked the wireless frequency of the demonstration and sought to enact maximum embarrassment. Marconi stayed quiet about the incident, but Fleming turned to the newspapers for help uncovering the perpetrator of this 'scientific hooliganism'. Maskelyne, the world's first wireless hacker, took pleasure in coming forward only a few days later.

Few of Marconi's triumphs were straightforward or uncontroversial. In December 1901 Marconi attempted, and claimed to have succeeded in, wirelessly transmitting across 3,540 km (2,200 mi.) of the North Atlantic between Poldhu (Cornwall, UK) and St John's, Newfoundland. Critics, then and now, believe that this was a technical impossibility at the time and suggest, kindly, that Marconi must have mistaken atmospheric interference for the Morse signals he claimed to have heard. What is more certain is that, again, Marconi had incorporated the inventions of others into his own apparatus without appropriate acknowledgement – in this case a mercury-based coherer with telephone adaptor that was almost identical to the semiconductor diode detector demonstrated by the Indian radio pioneer Jagadish Chandra Bose (1858–1937) in London in 1899. Marconi denied any such accusations, claiming instead to have been given the coherer by an acquaintance in the Italian navy. The precise details of the 'Italian Navy Coherer Scandal' remain controversial and contested to this day, particularly in India, although there is now widespread recognition of Bose's prior invention and his pioneering role in the invention of radio and the birth of electronics.

If Marconi had been rather too eager to hear what he wanted to hear across the North Atlantic, it was surely because he recognized that if wireless telegraphy was to be anything other than a scientific curiosity it required a clear commercial application. The wired telegraph system had extended around the world over the previous half century, connecting major commercial and strategic sites via a network of submarine and overland cables. It was fast, reliable, fairly cheap and protected by either vast commercial interests or, as in the United Kingdom, an impregnable state monopoly. Rather than compete with the wired telegraph, wire*less* telegraphy had the capacity to fill in the blank spaces on the communications map by connecting smaller and more isolated communities for whom a cable-based solution would be commercially unjustifiable. In 1898 Marconi was commissioned to link the Hawaiian Islands in just such an endeavour. And yet Marconi believed the true commercial potential lay further out at sea – linking the ever-expanding fleets of military and merchant ships that served the maritime routes of the British Empire and North Atlantic trade.

A Marconi operator
at work aboard
Titanic's sister
ship *Olympic.*

Ship-to-ship and ship-to-shore communications required wireless to
operate on an oceanic scale – a technological development that might
be helped along and given impetus with a thick slab of national moral
panic. In correspondence with *The Times*, Fleming made the case for
wireless:

> Wireless telegraphy will not take the place of telegraphy with wires.
> Each has a special field of operations of its own, but the public
> have a right to ask that the fullest advantage shall be taken of that
> particular service which ether-wave telegraphy can now render in
> promoting the greatest safety of those at sea, and that, in view of
> our enormous maritime interests, this country shall not permit
> itself to be outraced by others in the peaceful contest to apply
> the outcome of scientific investigations and discoveries . . . to the
> service of those who are obliged to face the perils of the seas.[26]

Fleming's letter had a galvanizing effect, as it was surely intended to, and
within days other correspondents had added to the growing clamour
in the London press. The message was consistent and resounding.

Indian physicist
and radio pioneer,
Jagadish Chandra
Bose (1858–1937).

Wireless could save lives and bring military advantage to the nation.
For Captain Baden Baden-Powell (a brother of Robert, founder of the
Scout movement), it was a matter of 'duty' to

> urge in every possible way the adoption of such a practical inven-
> tion, which would, without doubt, do so much to increase the
> fighting efficiency of our Navy, but which might any day mitigate
> or prevent accidents, collisions, and strandings at sea.[27]

Wireless was not only being talked of as a national priority, but had
been elevated, rhetorically at least, to the height of national service, with

Marconi at the helm as its publicist-in-chief. This elision of radio with national duty was further intensified during the two world wars, and reflected both the blurring of civilian and military life and the shifting role of women in war.

MUSIC, SOUND AND THE HUMAN VOICE

Until 1906, radio operated exclusively within the strange and secretive world of dots and dashes. Words needed to be encoded before they could be transmitted through the opening and closing of the telegrapher's key, and then, of course, decoded before they could be understood wherever they were received. In this sense, radio bore much more resemblance to the wired telegraph systems of Cooke and Wheatstone rather than the kind of broadcast radio we are most familiar with today.

Transmitting the human voice was much more complex. First, the voice needed to be converted into electrical impulses using the recently invented, although still rudimentary, 'microphone' (developed by David Hughes during the 1870s). Second, unlike the staccato electromagnetic pulses required to transmit Morse code (which could be produced by spark-gap transmitters), the continuous nature of the human voice required a mechanism for producing continuous radio waves. The Canadian inventor Reginald Fessenden (1866–1932) is credited with being the first person to successfully bring these innovations together. During the 1890s he developed a system for generating reliable and continuous radio waves (a high frequency, or HF, alternator) and, by 1900, was experimenting with ways to superimpose the sound from a microphone onto a radio wave and transmit the resulting signal. On Christmas Eve 1906, Fessenden was in a position to broadcast. After alerting nearby shipping to expect an important transmission, it is reported that Fessenden simply started to speak. Telegraph operators on ships in the North Atlantic and Caribbean, accustomed to interpreting squeaks of Morse from their headsets, were 'astonished'

'It's a woman's war too': radio as a gendered expression of wartime national duty.

The 'tomato can'
microphone used to
announce the results
of the Harding v.
Cox presidential
race, 1920.

to hear 'the unimaginable' tones of the human voice. In the spirit of a
true Christmas concert, Fessenden followed up with music from his
Edison phonograph, a rendition on the violin and Bible readings.[28]

In the years that followed, the invention and development of the
thermionic valve (first invented by J. A. Fleming in 1904) and amplifi-
cation technologies such as the audion tube (Lee de Forest, 1906)
would ensure that radio emerged as a viable system of broadcast communications. The first commercial broadcasting licences were issued
in the United States in 1920, and the first true commercial 'broadcast'
was the declaration of the Harding v. Cox presidential election result
on 11 November by KDKA in East Pittsburgh.

The sound quality of these early transmissions was an immediate
and ongoing concern for broadcasters and listeners due to the persistent
hum of static interference – a phenomenon familiar to any listeners
to medium-wave radio to this day. While many ideas were put forward
for the elimination of this noise, it was American electrical engineer
Edwin Howard Armstrong (1809–1954) who recognized the acoustic
benefits of superimposing the audio source onto the carrier radio wave

Edwin Armstrong
atop the WJZ
transmitter in
central New York
City, May 1923.

by modulating its frequency rather than its amplitude – a process
that would become known, of course, as 'FM' (Frequency Modulation)
as opposed to the more established 'AM' (Amplitude Modulation).
It would be a further twenty years (in 1940) before high-fidelity
FM broadcasts were commercially licensed in the United States. Perhaps unsurprisingly, even this final marker in the story of radio's early
development is laced with deceit and tragedy. Despite inventing technologies vital to the popularization of radio (for which he received
43 patents), a long-running dispute with the Radio Corporation of

Armstrong's experimental FM tower in Alpine, New Jersey, was built in 1938 and remains operational.

America and its powerful president, David Sarnoff (1891–1971), took a heavy financial and emotional toll on Armstrong. He committed suicide in 1954. For a man who had once revelled in performing handstands atop transmitter masts high above the New York skyline it was tragically fitting that he chose to end his life – dressed flawlessly in a hat, coat and leather gloves – by stepping from his thirteenth-floor apartment overlooking New York's East River and, once again, taking to the air.[29]

Armstrong's radio experimentations during the 1930s have left a lasting material legacy. The 125-m (410-ft) Alpine Tower, built by Armstrong on the shores of the Hudson River in 1938 for testing FM transmissions, is still actively used as radio transmitter mast and was critical in re-establishing television and FM radio services to New Yorkers following the collapse of the World Trade Center (and its rooftop radio antennae) on 11 September 2001.

3
RADIO AND
THE NATION

The nation with the most radio stations by far is the United States, with, according to recent figures from the Federal Communications Commission (FCC), 4,626 stations broadcasting on AM, a further 10,867 on FM and many more on satellite radio.[1] Turkey is a surprising, albeit distant, runner up with 1,090 radio stations broadcasting on a variety of different frequencies and bands. The UK has 280 digital radio stations – the world's largest digital radio network – and the government plans to move the country's 206 AM stations and 696 FM stations onto the digital network by about 2020. On the other end of the scale, even the smallest and most remote island nations have radio broadcasting systems. Kiribati's 104,000 inhabitants enjoy a choice of three radio stations, while the Micronesian state of Palau has six stations serving its 22,000 citizens. A peculiarly intense radio environment can be found in the Falkland Islands, a UK overseas territory in the South Atlantic Ocean, 644 km (400 mi.) or so off the coast of southern Argentina. There, the 3,600 Falkland Islanders and resident UK military personnel have a selection of six radio stations, including three from the British Forces Broadcasting Service (BFBS). Falklands Radio, the oldest and most popular station in the islands, broadcasts for 72 hours per week from Stanley, the islands' capital, and shares its frequencies with a local relay of the BBC's World Service. The growing diaspora of St Helenians who live and work on the islands can enjoy the sounds of home via 'Saint FM Community Radio', which is carried on the local satellite television network.

Radio Map of these United States

Showing KOIN *and affiliated Columbia Stations*

PRESENTED WITH THE COMPLIMENTS OF KOIN, INC., THE PORTLAND NEWS
"The feature station of the Great Northwest."

Benedict Anderson famously described the nation as an 'imagined community' – an entity to which many of us subscribe emotionally, culturally and socially even though, he notes, 'members of even the smallest nation will never know most of their fellow members, meet them, or even hear them, yet in the minds of each lives the image of their communion.' Anderson traces the origins of that image and that communion to the sixteenth century, with the birth of the printing press and printed materials that could spread ideas, philosophies, religious interpretation and political opinions further and faster than the physical movement of a particular philosopher, theologian or politician. By the eighteenth century, newspapers and novels further intensified the imaginative appeal of 'the nation' and, in the case

Mapping KOIN and Columbia stations across the United States, 1930.

of newspapers, routinized a weekly or daily re-engagement with a national collective. But the printed word had – and continues to have – its limitations, particularly in societies with strong oral traditions or where literacy is low, and it is in Anderson's acknowledgement of this limitation that he recognizes, albeit briefly, the potentialities for national imaginaries on the air. 'Invented only in 1895,' Anderson footnotes, 'radio made it possible to bypass print and summon into being an aural representation of the imagined community where the printed page scarcely penetrated.'[2]

Since the first radio broadcasts in the early 1920s, the modern nation state has been shaped through a close and even symbiotic relationship with technologies of mass communication. Radio had the power, for the first time in human history, to extend particular events, symbols and sounds across large parts of a national population in real time and all at once. Moments of celebration, commemoration and remembrance, sporting prowess and political intrigue; of high drama or the most everyday cultural practice – all were relayed through radio for hundreds, even thousands, of kilometres from their geographically specific points of happening. Radio produced national audiences, but also determined which events in a nation's cultural repertoire might be considered appropriate for national showcasing.

COMMUNITY IN THE AIR

Before radio could foster any kind of national community, however, the potential for radio waves to be harnessed for mass communication had to be determined – and even before it could be determined, it first had to be imagined. After all, for nearly a quarter of a century following radio's 'invention' in 1895, it operated almost entirely within a mysterious world of codes – usually Morse – and cyphers, and was a point-to-point form of communication between two identifiable operators. Even to use the term 'radio' in relation to this period is something of a historical misnomer. What we now know as radio waves were

most commonly referred to as Hertzian waves in the early years of the twentieth century, and the name 'radio' only really entered widespread usage, beginning in the United States, as a contraction of the commercial 'radio-telegraphy' services that began to emerge in the decade or so that followed. In Britain and the British Empire, where the term 'wireless telegraphy' was preferred and promoted by the Marconi Company, the natural contraction wasn't radio, but 'the wireless'. Although 'radio' was eventually triumphant on both sides of the Atlantic and globally, 'the wireless' was steadfastly preserved in some quarters of British society and continues to be deployed in certain British households to this day. It would be quite wrong, however, to mistake this defiant act of linguistic preservation as a straightforward example of anti-Americanism, or even as an act of linguistic nationalism in defence of a 'pure' British English. Instead, it is the product of another Great British obsession: class – with its specific origin in the 1954 publication of Nancy Mitford's essay 'The English Aristocracy' in *Encounter* magazine. In this now-infamous piece, the expatriated Mitford (she moved from London to Paris in 1945) provided a glossary of terms used by the English upper classes (which she termed 'U') alongside their lower-middle-class (or non-U)

A 'ham' operator with amateur radio equipment, *c.* 1921.

equivalents and in doing so provoked a somewhat anxious national debate about class-consciousness and the possibilities of a post-war meritocratic society. Alongside 'U'-appropriate words such as 'spectacles', 'lavatory', 'pudding', 'sofa' and 'napkin' (as opposed to 'glasses', 'toilet', 'sweet', 'couch' and 'serviette'), Mitford advocated 'the wireless' as a shibboleth for British upper-class acceptability – never, heaven forfend, to be confused with the distinctly non-U 'radio'.

Radio's implication in the secretive and somewhat 'coded' world of the British class system seems somewhat appropriate given radio's own technological origins. As with the telegraph, early radio was similarly point-to-point, transmitted in code and reliant on a skilled operator. Broadcasting for the masses this was not, but even in this somewhat furtive world of Morse code, radio would show itself capable of fostering communities of the air, albeit of a rather particular kind.

A young American learning to build his own radio, Brooklyn, *c.* 1922.

The early years of the twentieth century were a period of great radio freedom, opportunity and experimentation, and this freedom was not limited to the famous names that would come to dominate the burgeoning radio industry. Radio was equally the medium of choice for a substantial, if somewhat exclusive, group of radio enthusiasts and amateur experimenters who pushed radio's technical limits from within their own homes. Early images shared in publications such as the Marconi-produced *Wireless World* and the popular U.S. magazine *Radio News* (founded by the amateur wireless pioneer and, latterly, noted science fiction publisher Hugo Gernsback) reveal extraordinary arrays of large and small components, glass valves, metal casings, knobs and dials bound together with lengths of electrical wiring and occupying, in some cases, entire rooms or outbuildings. Rather than being an unassuming accessory to domestic life in the way that radio is today, domestic life was rather more often forced to fit around the alien-like presence of an amateur's wireless equipment.

Scenes like this, which were repeated across the United Kingdom, the United States, continental Europe, India and elsewhere represent the slightly awkward birth pangs of a new kind of community that would exist virtually and up in the air. This new band of 'etherites', as one magazine suggested they be called, would, as a matter of nightly routine, monitor the airwaves in the hope of detecting a signal transmitted by another experimenter, establish contact with that person, and repeat this process again and again in the hope of detecting experimenters over increasing distances. By the 1920s, the process of making 'contact' had become rather more formal than simply the exchange of Morse-coded messages. It was also becoming customary to exchange, via post, written confirmation of the electromagnetic encounter in the form of a so-called QSL card (QSL being radio 'Q' code for 'I confirm receipt of your transmission'), detailing the time, frequency, band, equipment used and a report of the reception quality.

The impact of this kind of radio was, of course, rather more profound than the simple matter of reconfiguring space within the home. It was creating new wireless communities of people who had, in most cases, never met one another face to face. As one experimenter in the British county of Wiltshire noted in an article published in *Wireless World*:

> My station is erected in the old club room of the Castle Inn . . . where our forefathers used to sit and drink the good ale brewed on the premises, and from which room communication with the outside world was only by means of a trapdoor, still in existence, through which the mystic password which allowed one to enter was whispered.

'Now', he continued, 'that magic password "wux" comes in through a piece of cable in the skylight.'[3]

By 1913, there were 2,000 such experimental stations across the United Kingdom and the air was beginning to fill with electromagnetic signals, although many of the stations were judged by the community to be 'excessively powerful' and displayed the disagreeable hallmarks of an 'untuned aerial'. Just as terrestrial communities require policing, so too did the new airborne communities of radio experimenters – especially with the prospect of war on the near horizon. Regulatory responsibility for experimental radio in the United States was granted to the Department of Commerce. In the United Kingdom, where radio was seen as a technological successor to the wired telegram (and, before that, the postal system), it was the Office of the Postmaster General. More informally, experimental transmissions were regulated through subscriptions to a growing number of radio clubs, which not only fostered discrete sub-national radio communities but sought to impose 'good practice' and 'radio discipline' within the larger community of experimental licence-holders.

Ham radio, the spiritual successor to pre-war 'experimental radio', continues to this day and is a popular hobby. There are an estimated 80,000 active amateur licence-holders in the UK, 16,000 in India and 717,000 in the United States. North Korea is noteworthy for having

1001 RADIO QUESTIONS and ANSWERS

COMPILED BY THE STAFF OF

RADIO NEWS

1930 EDITION

Price 50¢

EXPERIMENTER PUBLICATIONS INC., NEW YORK, N.Y.

no officially registered ham radio operators, although even the highly
secretive North Korean government has on occasions allowed international NGO workers to transmit while based in Pyongyang. Radio
'hams' continue to make contact with others in their own country but
derive particular enjoyment from establishing a verifiable connection
through the continuing exchange of QSL cards with users around the
world, over distances that would have been unimaginable to their interwar predecessors. This extraordinary spirit of internationalism was
celebrated in the words of the 1951 'CQ Serenade' (CQ being amateur
radio code for 'attention', used as an invitation for other listeners to
respond), composed by Maurice Durieux (1907–1976) although better-
known to the ham community by his callsign 'VE2QS'. Irrespective of
a person's physical location, whether in India, the United States, Canada,
France or the UK, for Durieux and other hams, radio transformed the
world into 'one great big party line'.[4]

For all this sense of radio freedom (a party line is a shared telephone
line rather than a party in the literal sense), access to the electromagnetic spectrum was much more limited for the radio hobbyists of the

1950s than it had been for the original wireless experimenters. Two world wars had cemented radio's status as a national asset to be used in the 'national interest', and had become almost inseparable from the affairs of peace and war.[5] Radio, additionally, had become a lucrative industry, driven by two parallel technological developments: first, the recently refined process for transmitting human voices and music through the air; second, the capacity to radiate those sounds out across vast areas for detection by multiple receivers. In short, the emergence of viable systems of 'broadcasting'.

NATION SHALL SPEAK UNTO NATION

'How many radio miles did you go last night . . . Did you voyage from New York to Chicago? Did you look in on Boston fifty seconds after and on Philadelphia half-a-minute after that? If not, why didn't you?'[6] These were the apparently 'up-to-the-minute' questions being asked of the American public when contemplating the purchase of a radio receiving set in 1924. Advertisements filled the pages of the popular magazines of the day and seemed to announce that radio had come of age. Much like the motor car, radio promised American citizens a new kind of mobility and a freedom to travel across the length and breadth of the United States, looking in on the major cities along the way. With the simple turn of a dial, purchasers of the De Forest 'D-12 Radiophone', for example, might even imagine being liberated from the Earth altogether, transported like the mythical Greek hero Bellerophon through the night sky on the back of the winged horse, Pegasus. If this was a fantasy of modernity and mythology, it was also an expression of authority and scientific expertise. The De Forest name etched into the brass plates on the front of the sideboard-sized 'D-12' signified the approval of Lee de Forest (1873–1961), the self-styled 'father of radio'. Other radio manufacturers promised to alleviate the torment of house-bound isolation brought on by the rigours of winter and the infirmities of old age. Others still promised to unite

A perfect travel companion – the portable Radiola. Advertisement from *National Geographic* magazine, 1927.

The outdoor days are coming...
get a Radiola that is portable!

WITH the outdoor days coming—the picnics and camp trips and tours—get a Radiola 26, that can forget it's a home set, and change in a moment to a portable, to carry the music and the sports news with you!

Radiola 26 is famous as a portable—it has traveled nearly half the world! But it is not just a portable. It is a six-tube super-heterodyne, finely made to the last screw—and beautifully cased in walnut. On the finest program, it is clear and real. In the smartest living room, it fits luxuriously.

And when the out-o'-door days

Radiola 26, with six Radiotrons. Finished in walnut; with a matching cabinet to hold home batteries or battery eliminators, and to make possible an antenna, if you wish one. $225.

come, your Radiola 26 cleverly fills a double purpose. Small portable batteries go inside the back. The loop is in the cover, and you need take along no antenna. The loudspeaker is built in. Just pick up the Radiola—and take it along. The separate cabinet is made to hold either batteries or battery eliminators, when you listen in at home.

It pays to get a Radiola 26—not only for fine performance—but for double service—and double value! Wherever you are, in a city skyscraper or a lonely mountain top, it goes with you—brings along the music and the news!

Buy with confidence **[Authorized Dealer]** *where you see this sign.*

KEEP IN TOUCH WITH YOUR FRIENDS AT SEA

POST OFFICE TELEGRAM OR RADIOTELEGRAM

send them

RADIOTELEGRAMS

SAMS · STAR

GPO

the generations through a shared passion for sport. 'It's great to get every word from the field – just as sharp and distinct as if you stood by the announcer,' the Radiola Company promised its prospective customers.[7] For all their different visual and textual appeals, these and other advertisements consistently reveal a transformation in the representation and 'popular culture' of radio in the immediate post-war period. Radios were now 'mainstream'; they fitted into your life and home, and certainly didn't require technical expertise to make them work. Radiolas were 'simple to operate',[8] Crosleys 'a delight' thanks to 'the real ease with which local stations may be tuned out'.[9] The De Forest teased customers with just a hint of the technical:

> We could be extremely technical in telling you how the four tubes do the work of seven and why the crystal detector gives both power and economy to this instrument. If you are technically inclined, we shall be glad to do so if you will write us.[10]

For everyone else, the appeal was simple: 'here is a Radiophone so astonishingly simple for the work it does that it's your best introduction to the marvels of radio space.'[11]

Radio was, for many, a new kind of space – and it was a space that was being stretched from cosmopolitan centres to cover entire nations. The editorial decisions and creativity of radio producers, administrators and executives played – and continue to play – an important part in defining, and refining, national values and qualities for the electronic era. During the 1930s, for example, the BBC seemed rather less interested in holding up a mirror to the nation than in fashioning its own particular version of 'Britishness' – a Britishness that seems, ironically, to have been inspired more by the Scottish Presbyterianism of the corporation's director-general, John Reith (1889–1971), than any true reflection of interwar Britain. Reith insisted on a somewhat formal, some might say 'starchy', presentational style (which included the radio announcers wearing full evening dress), while looking to the

De Forest promoted radio's ability to transport listeners across the United States; from *Radio Broadcast* magazine, December 1924.

BEAUTY

Drawn especially for Crosley Radio by Franklin Booth

You're there —with a CROSLEY

The NEW *Buddy*

Here is something entirely NEW in radio . . . . a real sensation . . . . a NEW and utterly exquisite mantel, clock or table type self-contained A. C. electric radio receiving set so light in weight and small in size as to be readily movable from place to place in the home. It can also be moved from house to house under the arm. It is especially ideal for efficiency apartments where space is at a premium. Contains the same type receiving set as The PAL and The MATE. Employs three Screen Grid tubes. Nothing ever equalled it at so low a price . . . . $64.50 WITH TUBES

BEAUTY . . . . hours of reverent music . . . . voices of bells, and the wing-beat of birds at dusk . . . . Yuletide carols . . . . an organ's soft, prayerful voice drifting out across miles of snow . . . . or the jolly greeting of Kriss Kringle himself, proclaiming to the world his love of little children. Beauty everywhere, in all lands . . . . a spiritual beauty, given life by the quality of a great organ in a centuried-old cathedral . . . . the orchestration of priceless bells that were ten years in the making.

RADIO . . . . it is the function of modern radio, at its best, to bring all these seasonal joys into our homes and to place YOU, at a moment's notice, in the very presence of the singer and the song. But, just as one bell is cast of surpassing quality of tone . . . . just as one organ may echo the master craftsman's skill and sympathetic understanding . . . . in this same manner there is a superlative in radio. CROSLEY ideals and quality live up to such high traditions.

THE CROSLEY RADIO CORPORATION
Powel Crosley, Jr., President   Home of "the Nation's Station"—WLW
CINCINNATI
Also manufacturers of CROSLEY Battery Radio Receiving Sets, the CROSLEY ROAMIO (manufacturer's built-in-factory-installed automobile radio), AMRAD RADIOS

CROSLEY RADIO

A Crosley Radio
Corporation
advertisement, 1927.

AMOS AND ANDY

Actors Charles Correll (left) and Freeman Gosden (right) in blackface as radio characters Amos 'n' Andy (1928–60).

socially acceptable events of London's cultural and sporting 'season' as the foundation for the BBC's programming. If British broadcasting looked characteristically 'stiff upper lip', radio in the United States was rather more unbridled. Popular music filled the airwaves while programmes such as *Amos 'n' Andy* – a sitcom that crudely portrayed Harlem's black community – surged in popularity and attracted millions of dollars in advertising revenue. Confirming the show's status as a modern American landmark, George Bernard Shaw is reported to have said, 'There are three things which I shall never forget about America – the Rocky Mountains, Niagara Falls, and "Amos 'n' Andy".'[12]

Structurally, too, the United States took a strikingly divergent path to the United Kingdom and the majority of Commonwealth countries in the development of 'professional' radio systems. As had happened with electric telegraph companies previously, profitability was the guiding motive behind the development of broadcasting companies in the U.S., and radio manufacturers such as the Radio Corporation of America (RCA) jostled for position to establish and acquire individual radio stations – most often in major cities – in order to connect them into more extensive and commercially power-ful broadcasting networks. Between 1923 and 1926, for example, RCA, backed by famous industrial names such as General Electric and Westinghouse, acquired the stations WEAF (New York) and WCAP (Washington, DC) from AT&T, a multinational entertainment conglomerate, and merged them with its existing broadcasting facil-ities. The result of these acquisitions and mergers was the National Broadcasting Company (NBC).

In Britain, the government took a more active hand in guiding radio's development, preferring that radio manufacturers worked in cooperation rather than competition to develop radio infrastructure. As a result, six of the leading radio manufacturers, eager to ensure that there was programming of sufficient quality to satisfy potential cus-tomers, formed a conglomeration to undertake broadcasting across the country. The enterprise gave rise to perhaps the most famous initials in world broadcasting – BBC – and to a rapid expansion in radio listening. Within six weeks of its official inaugural broadcast to London and the southeast of England in 1922, the British Broadcasting Company had pushed sales of radio receiver licences to almost 36,000. By the end of 1924, with twenty BBC broadcasting stations across the country, that figure had reached 1 million. By 1926, another 1.25 million listeners had been added to the BBC's ranks.

But this was not the public service British Broadcasting Corpo-ration familiar to us today. Instead, the British Broadcasting Company of the early 1920s was a commercial broadcaster that generated reve-nues from the sale of radio licences (undertaken by the General Post Office), but also through commercial sponsorship of its programming. If it hoped to succeed commercially, the BBC needed to both expand

A GPO Wireless
Investigation Service
van, designed to
detect radio licence
avoidance, c. 1920.

the reach of radio broadcasts throughout the UK to maximize potential listeners (and also subscribers), and also to demystify a medium that, for many, remained something of a technological unknown. On the cover of its first Christmas edition in 1923, the *Radio Times*, the BBC's own radio listings magazine, provided an important visual challenge to the perceived 'oddity' of radio. Gone were the elaborate wiring arrays, the glowing valves and stacks of QSL cards that had characterized an earlier set of wireless visions within the home. Radio was now smaller, sleeker, even stylish, and very much in keeping with the comforts of a modern household. Gone too was the solitary image of the middle-aged male body fine-tuning laboratory-like equipment; replaced instead with the image of a family preparing for the arrival of Christmas by sitting together and enjoying, we are told, 'a song at twilight'. But for all radio's increasingly subtle physical presence in the home, this wasn't yet a radio that could be allowed to passively blend into the

Radio at the centre
of domestic family
life: *Radio Times*,
December 1923.

background of family life – the imagery is much more active than that. While the family's chairs may be pointing towards the warming glow of the family hearth, their heads and bodies are visibly drawn towards the radio in a pose of active, enthralled, perhaps even silent, radio listening. The symbolism of this reorientation, even if unintended by this and other artists, illustrators and photographers during this period, is striking. While the scene is unquestionably benign and homely, perhaps what we also see here is a representation of radio's power – it's power to enthral and entertain, to reconfigure and reorient the household, but also its power to invisibly connect individuals, families and the home itself into an expanding and national radio infrastructure. In that sense, perhaps what this image also symbolizes is a certain kind of loss – of privacy and even a certain kind of domestic sovereignty – as radio claimed a little bit of the home for the public realm.

Other models for broadcasting were pursued throughout Europe and beyond. In India, the British model of state monopoly was adopted in 1930, albeit with more limited penetration into the subcontinent's vast population due to the sole use of English as the national broadcast language. In Germany, Hitler's brand of National Socialism had brought the Nazi Party to power in 1933, and although broadcasting had a negligible role in securing that victory it was immediately embraced as an essential instrument of Nazi governance. Speaking at the opening of the 'International Radio Exhibition' in Berlin in August 1933, Joseph Goebbels, Hitler's propagandist-in-chief, described radio as 'the eighth great power . . . the most influential and important intermediary between a spiritual movement and the nation, between the idea and the people'. But he also determined that this was a medium that needed to be harnessed, subordinated and inscribed with a clearly expressed direction. It required, in other words, a clear voice and unambiguous message:

> We want a radio that reaches the people, a radio that works for the people, a radio that is an intermediary between the government and the nation, a radio that also reaches across our borders to give the world a picture of our character, our life, and our work.[13]

The realities were, of course, somewhat darker. Radio was to become not only a servant to the German state and people, but a vital pillar through which the political authority of the Third Reich was realized, practised and enforced. 'All of Germany hears the Führer with the Peoples' Receiver,' announced one Nazi poster from 1936. Listening was not an option; it was a national duty. The mass production of the Volksempfänger VE301, the People's Receiver, made the

technology for receiving radio broadcasts affordable to the masses for
the first time, although not all broadcasts would, or could, be received.
Many models of the VE301 and its successor the DKE38, often referred
to as Goebbels-Schnauze (Goebbel's snout) were adapted to restrict
access to non-Nazi frequencies. Speaking while giving evidence during
the Nuremberg trials in August 1946, Albert Speer, Hitler's architect
and armaments minister reflected on Hitler's domination of German
political life and radio's role in fashioning a thoroughly abusive and
securitized relationship between the state and its citizenry:

> Hitler's dictatorship differed in one fundamental point from all its
> predecessors in history. His was the first dictatorship in the present
> period of modern technical development, a dictatorship which
> made complete use of all technical means in a perfect manner for
> the domination of its own nation.
>
> Through technical devices such as radio and loudspeaker,
> 80 million people were deprived of independent thought. It was
> thereby possible to subject them to the will of one man ... Also,
> one of the results was a far-reaching supervision of the citizen
> of the state and the maintenance of a high degree of secrecy for
> criminal events.[14]

THE NATIONAL HERALD

Among the many radio-related observations offered by the celebrated
media theorist Marshall McLuhan, he noted that radio is intimately
woven into human experience of space and expressions of territorial-
ity. Radio's sounds, he suggested, have an 'unrivaled power to shape
and pattern their own unique space', functioning as a national, even
global, 'Tribal Drum'.[15] Taking inspiration from the natural world, he
suggested that radio could be usefully imagined as electronic 'bird song'
– a sound that is neither a straightforwardly impulsive nor emotional
expression, but a sonic strategy employed by a living creature to

Goebbels relays
the Führer's New
Year message to the
German people in
January 1936.

acoustically produce and define an occupied space; its territory. In much
the same way, he argued, the traditional tribal drum served the dual
function of beating out an acoustic perimeter to a physical tribal homeland while also signifying, through its rhythms and cadences, the tribe's
subscription to a shared identity, a particular set of shared values and
unified 'codes of law'. These 'acoustic spaces' further chime with religious 'sounding devices' such as church bells which, day or night, were
capable of sounding out the furthest limits of a particular community,
or indeed the worldly extent of Christendom. 'Those who could hear
the bells were in the parish,' noted the acoustic ecologist R. Murray
Shafer, 'those who could not were in the wilderness.'[16]

The presence or absence of radio sound is a peculiarly twentieth-
century and electromagnetic marker of this kind of inclusion or
exclusion. Rather like the nation itself, radio can be read, heard and
experienced as a metaphorical 'container' – reinforcing the shared
and common values of those within its earshot to the exclusion of
those beyond. It is perhaps little surprise, then, that 'the radio' and
'the nation' became so intimately linked as ideas and 'objects' during

Ganz Deutschland
hört den Führer

mit dem Volksempfänger

143

'All Germany listens
to the Führer with
the People's Radio':
promoting the
Volksempfänger
VE301.

the early twentieth century. Possibly somewhat wishfully, radio was given the status of an instrument – *the* instrument – with the potential to bind long-established nations into closer and more meaningful communion, a 'new social space unifying the nation' while, simultaneously, buttressing it against new social and economic challenges. 'There was something about radio waves and their impervious mobility across social boundaries', note Michele Hilmes and Jason Loviglio, 'that served as an ideal symbol for national togetherness.'[17]

McLuhan's metaphorical flourishes suggest a strategic as well as symbolic connection between radio and nation. At his most discomfiting, he labels radio as 'the architect of lebensraum', in an apparent reference to radio's skill in occupying and enclosing space (literally a 'space for life' in German) – in the air and on the ground.[18] Radio, in this way, isn't simply a tool of national cohesion and coalescence; it is also expansionist and invested with a colonial-like impulse to advance along an electronic frontier. Although the connection is left unmade, it is perhaps inevitable that McLuhan's choice of words serves to connect radio with the particular expansionary impulses of Nazi strategy during the 1930s and 1940s. This is a connection that obscures as much as its reveals, particularly given the role that radio was to play in the post-colonial transition of emergent African states, in the partition and independences of South Asia, and in building a post-war 'homeland' for Jews in Israel.

During the evening of 29 November 1947, news from New York that would fundamentally reconfigure the map of the Middle East was relayed via radio receivers across the ancient city of Jerusalem. Following months of investigations, interviews and hearings, the production of dozens of maps and the publication of a proposal to divide Mandatory Palestine into Jewish and Arab states, the moment had come for the United Nations to vote on Resolution 181. Inside the UN's temporary headquarters – a repurposed gyroscope factory in the New York suburb of Lake Success – diplomats still wrangled to shore up support from the 56 member states. Reluctant delegates were reportedly dragged from lavatory cubicles to ensure their votes were cast in support or opposition to the motion. For those listening to the unfolding events via their radios in Jerusalem, the tension was almost unbearable. For many, the voting by the UN 'jury' rendered the Yishuv community (the Jewish community in Palestine) as defendants in a kind of electromagnetic trial, passively awaiting a verdict that would have the most fundamental implications for their survival. This particular Jewish audience was, in reality, rather less than passive. In an era before radio 'phone-ins', the broadcast from New York activated minds and bodies. It was not uncommon for individual listeners, or households, to busily scribble down their own running total of the votes as they were announced over the radio, recalculating the odds of success or failure in real time. Each result was discussed and debated. Not only were listeners active, they belonged to a listenership that was itself activated through their collective participation in the act of listening. As the votes were announced, there was a growing sense within the Yishuv that they were engaged in a shared experience within and between an imagined community of likeminded individuals with whom their futures were closely intertwined. This was an imagined community which, during that long evening in November, became something of a tangible reality. Due in part to the scarcity of radios, but mostly because of a common wish to share in the drama of the event, the fragmented radio community of individual listeners and households poured onto the dimly lit streets of Jerusalem and Tel Aviv in order to listen, collectively, to the announcement that a 'Hebrew State' (as David Ben-Gurion would describe it sometime later) had been voted into reality. The prominent Israeli author Amos Oz, who was only eight years old at the time, later recalled the radio drama unfolding from his position outside the family home in Jerusalem:

> The whole crowd seemed to have been turned to stone in that frightening night silence, as if they were not real people but hundreds of dark silhouettes painted onto the canvas of the flickering

Crowds celebrate the UN vote to partition Palestine in Tel Aviv, November 1947.

darkness. As though they had died on their feet. Not a word was heard, not a cough or a footstep. No mosquito hummed. Only the deep, rough voice of the American presenter blaring from the radio, which was set at full volume and made the night air tremble, or it may have been the voice of the president of the Assembly, the Brazilian Oswaldo Aranha. One after another he read out the names of the last countries on the list, in English alphabetical order followed immediately by the reply of their representative. United Kingdom: abstains. Union of Soviet Socialist Republics: yes. United States: yes. Uruguay: yes. Venezuela: yes. Yemen: no. Yugoslavia: abstains.

At that the voice suddenly stopped, and an otherworldly silence descended and froze the scene, a terrified, panic-stricken silence, a silence of hundreds of people holding their breath, such as I have never heard in my life either before or after that night. Then the thick, slightly hoarse voice came back, shaking the air as it summed up with a rough dryness brimming with excitement: Thirty-three for. Thirteen against. Ten abstentions and one country absent from the vote. The resolution is approved.[19]

In *Midnight's Children* (1981) Salman Rushdie portrays India's independence as the birth of a nation 'which would never exist except by the efforts of a phenomenal collective will – except in a dream we all agreed to dream'. Radio gave some semblance of form to that dream, and, for Rushdie, the 'magic of radio' is itself given form in the body of this story's main protagonist, Saleem. Saleem, born on the eve of India's midnight awaking, is gifted the ability to translate all of India's many languages. He becomes, in Rushdie's words, 'a sort of radio' – 'All India Radio' – receiving and transmitting messages and becoming a somewhat dreamlike 'national network' of shared thoughts and conversations. Radio, through Saleem, becomes emblematic of India's national unity pre-1947. But if radio was a technology of national consolidation, it was equally subject to the new nationalisms of partition, and new lines on the map of South Asia. When Saleem crosses into Pakistan, his 'inner ear radio' loses its ability to receive, the radio waves somehow jammed by the new border that imposes itself on the ground and in the ether.

Rushdie's magical realist use of radio as a guiding metaphor for exploring India's partition is rooted in the very real events of August 1947. 'At the stroke of the midnight hour, when the world sleeps, India will awake to life and freedom.' Jawaharlal Nehru's thin voice, clipped with Anglicization, seared through the massed assembly of dignitaries gathered in New Delhi's Council House and announced the moment that India, newly independent, would realize its tryst with destiny. Amplified by the array of microphones positioned in front of the lectern, Nehru's words were relayed to the large crowds gathered outside on New Delhi's grand boulevards and, via the national broadcaster, All India Radio – AIR – to the furthest geographical reaches of the new

nation. Twenty-four hours earlier, Mohammed Ali Jinnah had taken
to the airwaves of Radio Pakistan to announce, in not dissimilar terms,
'the fulfilment of the destiny of the Muslim nation'. Radio, which had
been established by the British with an eye (or an ear) to promoting
the unity of British India, had become the outspoken herald of its
fragmentation into India and Pakistan. For the Yishuv in Mandatory
Palestine, the message delivered by the midnight broadcast was somewhat less straightforward, the link between radio and nation more
tentative and fractious. As Tamar Liebes has recognized, the act of
listening live and all at once to a broadcast, to an event, so fraught
with uncertainty was, for the Jewish people, transformative, joyous
and a 'symbolic victory' over the still-emerging atrocities of Nazism.[20]
And yet, the silences and roars that greeted the news from the UN were
not, to Amos Oz's recollection, those of straightforward joy, but tinted
instead with 'horror and bewilderment'; a 'cataclysmic shout'.[21] Radio
had heralded the creation of a new State, but equally a new state of
uncertainty that would lead irrevocably to war.

NATIONAL AIR

If radio has worked to contain the nation through the 'sounding out' of
national identities, the nation hasn't always been the natural container
for radio. Like the air through which they propagate, radio waves are
no respecters of national borders, silently moving through airspace
with a complete disregard for sovereignty rooted in terra firma. It was
radio's capacity to move freely through the air that inspired Marconi's
experimental transmissions across the Atlantic, but it was these same
qualities that had, by the 1920s, focused attention onto radio's greatest
technical challenge. Left unchecked and unregulated, Europe's airspace had become thick with a chaotic noise of electromagnetic signals
and interference. Transmissions from Britain interfered with those in
northern France, Belgium and Denmark, while those from Luxemburg
hampered audibility in Germany, Belgium and France. If radio was to

be made to work as a communications system, then it was a system that needed careful regulation – and that required multinational agreements.

Beginning in 1925 and published in 1926, the so-called 'Geneva Plan' did exactly that, proposing specific frequencies to be allocated to signatory nations. Although the plan was partially ignored by the signatories, rejected altogether by the Soviet Union, and abused by the continuing broadcasts of Radio Luxembourg, the Geneva Plan clarified the need for the electromagnetic spectrum to be administered through broad international consensus – a task now undertaken by the International Telecommunication Union (ITU), a body of the UN. It had other effects, too. Radio, or more specifically the electromagnetic spectrum, might have been made subject to international agreement, but that agreement linked substantial sections of the spectrum to individual countries. Radio was confirmed as a treasured and precious national resource – one that national governments increasingly sought to manage and regulate, and others sought to challenge.

Illegal radio stations might be most readily associated with the 1960s, but the first 'radio pirate' was almost certainly Captain Leonard Plugge (1889–1981), a somewhat eccentric English engineer-cum-entrepreneur who bankrolled the creation of Radio Normandie in 1926. Broadcasting from the fishing port of Fécamp near Dieppe in northern France, the English-language broadcasts of Radio Normandie could be heard throughout the southern counties of England (and as far south as the French midlands), where it built a considerable listenership – especially so on Sundays when the BBC's schedule of religious programming and serious talks was at its most Reithian. Normandie's combination of relaxed chat and popular dance music provided an intoxicating and popular challenge to the BBC's rather more 'dry' offering, and is held at least partly responsible for Sir John Reith's resignation from the BBC in 1938. Plugge's activities had also paved the way for other more well-known 'border-busting' stations such as Radio Luxembourg, which broadcast from the Grand Duchy into the

United Kingdom for almost sixty years, from 1933 until 1992, only silenced during Europe's Nazi occupation during the Second World War. The U.S. had its own particular issues with border-busting radio during the 1930s. The most prominent case involved the self-styled 'Dr' John R. Brinkley (1885–1942), who dispensed highly questionable medical advice via his own high-powered radio station, XERA, located in Ciudad Acuña (Acuna City) on the U.S.–Mexico border. Brinkley's transmitters were located within, and were licensed by, Mexico, which only lightly regulated broadcast content – although the studio from which Brinkley broadcast, and his intended audience, was on the U.S. side of the border. Although unable to regulate Brinkley's transmissions emanating from Mexico, the U.S. Congress were nonetheless able to stifle his broadcasts by introducing an effective ban on the use of international telephone cables for the purpose of electromagnetic transmission in another country if those transmissions could be consistently heard within the U.S. The so-called Brinkley Act (1934) remains on the statute book to this day.

By the 1960s, the UK and other European countries were facing a renewed aerial challenge – albeit with uncharacteristically watery origins. Unlike Radio Normandie and Radio Luxembourg, which had taken advantage of differing broadcast legislation between neighbouring European states, a new generation of radio entrepreneurs had taken the concept of 'offshore' broadcasts rather more literally and constructed radio stations within decommissioned ferries and former fishing vessels, which were then anchored around the coastline of the target country. Others were constructed on disused sea forts originally designed to defend the UK's southern coastline from enemy invasion in wartime. Radio Caroline was the first, and remains the most famous, of the 'pirate radio' stations – so named, of course, because of their illicit maritime activities. Founded in 1964 as a direct challenge to the still unbearably stuffy offering of the BBC's 'light programme', Radio Caroline brought a daily dose of irreverent conversation and the latest in popular music to large swathes of the UK thanks to the

careful positioning of two radio ships – one anchored off the coast of Essex in the North Sea, the other moored near the Isle of Man in the Irish Sea. With such weak competition from the licence-fee funded BBC, Radio Caroline reached a regular audience of more than 10 million by the mid-1960s. Other pirate stations were making a splash too. Radio London – which broadcast from a decommissioned U.S. navy minesweeper also moored off the coast of Essex, and whose presenters included the likes of Tony Blackburn and Kenny Everett – persuaded

Radio pirates:
the DJs of Radio
Caroline sheltering
during a storm in
January 1966.

the Beatles to grant them exclusive broadcast rights to the new *Sgt. Pepper* album for eight days prior to its official release in June 1967. Other noteworthy stations included Radio Scotland, Radio 270 and Radio 390.

The pirate radio stations had a transformative effort on UK law and popular culture. In August 1967, the UK parliament passed legislation that not only extended UK legal jurisdiction beyond UK territorial waters and 'airspace', but made it illegal for any British subject to help or support unlicensed broadcasting activities, while also making it illegal to listen to unlicensed broadcasts within the UK. The BBC also responded, by instituting the most substantial reorganization of its radio output since its formation in 1922 in the hope of better reflecting the radio-listening habits of the UK population. The 'exciting new sound' of Radio 1 was certainly both 'exciting' and 'new' for the

MV *Ross Revenge*,
home of Radio
Caroline (1983–91).

BBC, but listeners could hardly fail to notice that many of the voices
– including those of Blackburn and Everett – were wholly familiar,
having become radio celebrities out at sea on the pirate-radio ships of
Radio London and Radio Caroline. Robbed of their stars, and with
ship-to-shore logistics made legally treacherous, the pirate stations
succumbed one-by-one until only Radio Caroline was left broadcasting, seemingly buoyed by its singular protest against the government
and increasingly subject to harassment by the UK authorities.

Although 'pirate radio' has been substantially defined in relation
to the restrictive broadcasting legislation of the United Kingdom from
the 1930s to the 1970s, it is an international phenomenon that continues
to this day. Israel had multiple pirate radio stations broadcasting from
ships located in the eastern Mediterranean throughout the 1970s and
1980s, most notably the Voice of Peace – although broadcasts came
to a rather sudden end in November 1993 when its host vessel, the MV
Peace was intentionally scuttled by its owner, the Israeli peace activist
Abie Nathan (1927–2008), following the signing of the Oslo Peace
Accords. In the United States, comparatively liberal broadcast regulations and a dynamic commercial radio market somewhat subdued the
requirement for alternative, pirate radio stations. As Matt Mason has
suggested, 'the gap between pirate radio stations in Europe and the
United States is almost as wide as the Atlantic itself.' Whereas radio
piracy was 'big business' in European waters, in the U.S. 'most pirates
have traditionally been fun, quirky operations run by hobbyists.'[22] Since
the Federal Communications Commission's (FCC) elimination of 'class
D' broadcast licences in 1979 (which forced many schools, churches,
clubs and community groups to close their low-power radio stations),
radio piracy in the U.S. has grown steadily. Today, pirate radio stations
in the U.S. are predominantly land-based (rather than maritime) and
found in the large urban centres, including New York, Boston, Los
Angeles and San Francisco, often catering to highly specific musical
tastes or specific language and ethnic groups in Spanish or Haitian
Creole. The New York borough of Brooklyn is a renowned radio-piracy

hotspot, hosting approximately thirty pirate radio stations. Reflecting the diverse ethnic and religious communities of the borough, illicit broadcasts of Caribbean music (especially during the warm summer months) compete with Latino stations and an increasingly vocal band of orthodox Jewish radio pirates for pre-eminence in the airwaves.

4
EMPIRES OF THE AIR

As early as 1910, the influential Cubist painter Robert Delaunay reflected on the new opportunities afforded by radio in his impressionistic paintings of Paris. As with many other artists, including Picasso, Delaunay considered the Eiffel Tower to be profoundly symbolic of the forces of early twentieth-century modernism. For Delaunay, though, the Eiffel Tower's interjection through the Parisian skyline was not only of a physical kind; it was profoundly elemental, even ethereal, and coupled to the tower's new-found association with the forces of electromagnetism: light and radio waves. In *Eiffel Tower with Trees* (*Tour Eiffel aux arbres*, 1910), which now hangs in the Guggenheim in New York, Delaunay plays with the liveliness of the Eiffel Tower in time and space through a deliberate contortion of perspective that reveals the tower from multiple perspectives at once, thereby putting the object into a kind of visual motion. The solid structure of the tower is further fractured through the interjection of 'light', shattering the once-solid elements into a kaleidoscope of component parts. The Eiffel Tower's capacities as a radio tower was, for Delaunay, especially suggestive, rather less for any kind of architectural dominance of the landscape of Paris, but because in radio Delaunay and other modernist artists and thinkers saw a potential mechanism for forging new kinds of communities, breaking down old barriers of distance, and transforming Europe into a forward-looking and global community.

From almost the moment of radio's discovery, it was adopted as an object, a technology and, ultimately, as a space with fantastical possibilities. Marconi, as we have already seen, dreamt of collapsing the expanse of the oceans, but, through the pages of the publicity magazine *Wireless World*, also imagined radio to be a new mechanism for governing in the air – an electromagnetic counterpoint to the Gothic spires of the Houses of Parliament, with particular 'power over the elements and forces of Nature', and with the capacity to both 'annihilate space' and reassert 'colonial ties'.[1] Others saw radio as a fuller expression of 'the nation' and a means to connect citizens more fully and comprehensively with the institutions, practices and rhythms of the state. Beginning in 1933, during the height of the Great Depression, U.S. President Franklin D. Roosevelt embraced the power of radio to communicate directly and simultaneously with the American people in the hope of quelling rumours, dispensing much-needed reassurance and providing an explanation for his more radical policy reforms. The inaugural 'fireside chat' on 12 March 1933 was a great success and established a pattern for presidential communications that would be repeated a further thirty times during Roosevelt's twelve-year presidency. In post-revolutionary Mexico, radio was imagined as a tool of education, social 'uplift' and the 'construction of nationality', although in Belgium radio seemed to represent Francophone cultural dominance as much as it represented the potential 'emancipator' of the Flemish people.[2] The world over, radio was bound up with ideological desires to connect people and places wirelessly, instantaneously and over vast geographical distances.

Writing in the late 1980s, the geographer David Harvey would give a name to the elision of spatial and temporal distance: 'time-space compression'. While Harvey intended this concept to inform a broader critique of capitalism and its push to create and exploit markets and workers, others have seen radio as rather more emancipatory. Some, including the media historian David Hendy, have argued that radio was integral to the 'rewiring' of the modern mind; turning

President Roosevelt used his 'fireside chats' to speak informally to American citizens during the Great Depression.

attention towards the sky and the 'air' – often using the metaphor of 'the ether' – as a medium with a near-utopian capacity to unite communities and secure peaceful international relations.[3] In the aftermath of the First World War, the Belgian *Radio* magazine imagined radio fashioning a 'brotherhood of mankind' and the creation of 'a super radio station' so powerful that it could 'call to the whole world'.[4] With the discovery and development of shortwave broadcasting beginning in the 1920s, the 'borderless' transmission of the human voice became rather less speculative. And yet, just as belief in the all-embracing ether came to be challenged by advances in the atmospheric sciences, so too were these utopian hopes and visions for radio and a benevolent international community of the air challenged by the dominant geometries of power that would come to shape the geopolitical world in the twentieth century.

Robert Delaunay, *Eiffel Tower with Trees*, 1910, oil on canvas.

RADIO FIRE

The development of viable systems for transmitting short-wavelength waves (that is, radio waves with wavelengths of between roughly 10 and 160 m, or 33 and 525 ft) was critical in the emergence of radio as a truly global technology capable of not just transmitting codes across oceans, but the human voice across entire continents and hemispheres. In the right – or, indeed, the wrong – hands, shortwave (sw) radio signals could ricochet between the Earth's surface and its atmosphere, carrying news, information and music to listeners thousands of kilometres from the source of the transmission. While this might seem to be the near-ultimate expression of modernist hopes for global community-building, the reality was that the expense of constructing shortwave stations would ensure that it remained in the hands of powerful commercial operators and national governments.

Amid the geopolitical turbulence of the interwar period, national governments were eager to exploit shortwave's strategic potentialities to educate, inform and persuade well beyond their own borders. The privately owned shortwave station PCJJ (owned by the Phillips company in the Netherlands) began broadcasting in Dutch to the Dutch East Indies (now Indonesia) in 1927, and in English, French and German to the rest of the world. The government-run Radio Moscow launched its sw transmissions in early 1929 and over the following twelve months began broadcasting programmes to audiences in Europe, North and South America, the Middle East and Japan, in German (initially), followed by French and English. The French government was so incensed by this perceived breach of sovereignty that it appealed to the League of Nations to have Radio Moscow's French broadcasts shut down, although it is interesting to note that the League of Nations itself became an international broadcaster in 1932.[5] Over the following decade border-crossing radio and propaganda would become a fact of life in Europe. The airwaves were emerging as a battlefield of ideas and ideologies, dominated, as James Wood notes, by 'the four big players, Britain, Germany, Italy and the USSR, [representing] British imperialism, German national socialism, fascism and communism respectively'.[6]

The Italian Futurist movement embraced radio as a guiding metaphor and source of intellectual-artistic inspiration during the 1920s–30s – a perfect crystallization, perhaps, of their fascination for speed, movement, technology, industry, youthfulness (and the detestation of anything old or traditional) and the conquest of space and time. The motion of radio waves, the behaviour of subatomic particles and the actions of devices such as the thermionic valve (considered to be the first electronic device and integral to the detection of electromagnetic waves) inspired Futurist leaders Filippo Tommaso Marinetti and Pino Masnata in their *Radio Manifesto* (1933) and other unpublished works.[7] As well as seeking the destruction of anything considered 'traditional', the Futurists saw radio as a central pillar in a project for the pursuit of new, pure modes of artistic expression that would, they claimed, abolish the theatre, the cinema, backward-looking audiences and even time itself. Radio, or *La Radia* as Marinetti and Masnata termed their perfected version of the technology, was, among other things, 'destined to increase the creative genius of the Italian race a hundredfold', while also abolishing, curiously, 'the ancient, tormenting nostalgia for faraway places':

> The possibility of picking up radio broadcasts from stations in different time zones, together with the absence of light, destroys the hours, the day, and the night. Reception and amplification, by means of thermionic valves, of light and of voices from the past, will destroy the concept of time.[8]

Marinetti and Masnata codified a range of powerful linguistic and visual motifs that can be traced through Futurist art back and forward from the manifesto's publication in 1933. A violently pulsating yet disassembled radio, with glowing thermionic valve and ferrous streak of electromagnetic energy, is the central feature of Fortunato Depero's

The 'radio listening
room' of Casa
Zampini, a product
of Italian Futurist
architectural design.

(1892–1960) *Radio Fire* (1922), with the destructive and regenerative
capacities of that same electromagnetic streak more vividly shown in
The Lightning Conductor (1926). Shortly after the publication of the
manifesto, Marinetti's wife, Benedetta Cappa Marinetti, was commissioned to paint a set of wall murals for the walls of the Palermo
post office. The resulting *Synthesis of Radio Communications* (1933–4)
depicts an elegant but also brutally industrial radio mast striking into
the heavens and bridging the turbulent and wave-filled space between
Earth and the upper atmosphere.

　　Whether or not the Futurists' vision for *La Radia* was destined to
occupy the 'immensity of space', as claimed by Marinetti and Masnata,[9]
some have heard in these words the spiritual beginnings of the time- and
space-altering properties of the Internet and the digital freedoms associated with the World Wide Web. It is difficult, however, to disassociate
La Radia from Marinetti's (and the Futurist movement's) political
entanglements with the rise of Italian nationalism, militarization and
'air power', for which they were renowned cheerleaders. The manifesto's
authoritarian and somewhat hectoring tone, and its talk of abolishing
institutions with which the Futurists disagreed, certainly reveal something of the movement's fascist sympathies. More vividly and directly,
the 1933 manifesto offers a sinister echo of the ethnic and racialized
legislation adopted by the recently elected National Socialist government in Germany. Radio had been, according to Marinetti and Masnata,
'trivialized by music' and now found itself in a 'repulsive state of languid,
negro monotony'. The Jews were an even more direct target. In outlining
a vision for 'going beyond patriotism' (which would require patriotism
to become the 'authentic religion of the Nation'), the Futurists issued
'a warning to Semites' – a demand that Jews 'identify themselves with
specific countries or risk expulsion'.[10] The Futurists and their vision for
radio had much more in common with the Nazis' Nuremberg Laws
than the modernists' utopian vision for a shared community in, and
of, the air.

DOMINION IN THE ETHER

On 19 December 1932, at precisely 9.30 a.m., the British Broadcasting
Corporation went global. Beginning with the easternmost flanks of
the British Empire, the great men of British broadcasting – that is to
say, the BBC's chairman, A. H. Whitely, and director-general, John
Reith – welcomed listeners to the inaugural transmission of the newly
formed Empire Service. Speaking from the BBC's Broadcasting House
in central London, Reith and Whitely delivered a distinctly starchy
message, initially to the English-speaking peoples of New Zealand and
Australia. The two men soberly repeated their live double act another
four times over the next fifteen-and-a-half hours for the benefit of
listeners in India, the Middle East, eastern and southern Africa, Canada
and the Caribbean. It was a momentous occasion that bound the furthest reaches of the British Empire into a continuous electromagnetic
endeavour. It was also an occasion loaded with uncertainties. Reith was
audibly wary about forecasting the future significance of broadcasting
to the empire. He was even more reserved in his judgement on the
quality of the programming that would be transmitted. 'Don't expect
too much in the early days,' he cautioned, 'the programmes will neither
be very interesting nor very good.' While this kind of straightforward-
ness might now be unthinkable in the modern era of broadcasting,
Reith's words reveal a profound uncertainty and even unease at the
BBC's new international mission. Broadcasting to the British Empire
would require considerable investment in experimental technologies
and practices, and new mechanisms for engaging with empire audiences and the wider world. Programmes would require a new kind of
language, new codes, routines and broadcasting conventions if they
hoped to achieve popularity in territories as diverse as New Zealand
and the West Indies, and in Dominions like Canada where listeners
were already developing a taste for commercial radio output from the
United States. The empire was also changing. The Statute of
Westminster (1931) ensured that Australia, Canada, New Zealand and

South Africa joined the United Kingdom in a federation of equals under the Crown. By contrast, the civil disobedience movements co-ordinated by Gandhi and the Indian National Congress had led to the denial of Dominion status for India, and a significant worsening in Anglo-Indian relations. Against this shifting, and often-violent, imperial backdrop, empire-wide broadcasting was lauded as a potential golden opportunity for enhanced imperial communication, coordination and mutual understanding. The BBC Empire Service, as well as being the voice of the colonial master, would also need to serve as a renewed source of imperial unity and inclusivity.

Another such institution was the monarchy, and in particular a monarch that was savvy to the potentialities of the modern broadcast media. The king, George V, would prove reluctant to embrace the 'radio age'. Beginning initially in 1923, John Reith had sought to persuade Buckingham Palace of the value of the monarch directly addressing the peoples of the empire over the airwaves, albeit with little success. The king consistently refused the BBC's invitations – due, it would seem, to a self-perceived lack of talent for public speaking and an apparent phobia of all things technological. The monarch remained obdurate in his refusal even after he took possession of his first radio receiver in 1924 – a gift from the BBC – and began listening avidly to the news service. This is not to suggest that the king's voice was absent from the radios of the British Empire altogether. Speeches delivered at opening ceremonies and other important occasions were recorded and distributed by the BBC to broadcasting stations throughout the empire. Some of these recordings attracted empire-wide audiences of over 10 million listeners, a record at the time. But despite this popularity, neither the BBC nor the monarch's closest advisers were able to persuade the king to deliver a personal message (as opposed to a formal speech) to his subjects via the radio. The passing into law of the Statute of Westminster proved, eventually, to be the catalyst that was required to change the king's mind, and only six days after the Empire Service's inaugural global relay, on Christmas Day 1932, George V delivered the first personal message from the monarch to the peoples of Britain and the empire.

If Reith's inaugural broadcast had been apologetic and tentative, the king's message was a celebration of radio's emerging achievements and potentialities. The preparations for the speech had, in themselves, been an exercise in technical and logistical brilliance. Notwithstanding the elegant composition of the official portrait, the king, who was spending Christmas at his private house at Sandringham, would, in reality, speak from a makeshift studio constructed in a small boxroom tucked under the grand staircase of the royal dwelling. Two further rooms were temporarily filled with amplifiers and other broadcasting equipment. The microphones at Sandringham were connected through Post Office landlines to the control room at the BBC's Broadcasting House in central London. From there, the speech was transmitted via the BBC Home Service, and then relayed through the Empire Broadcasting Station's shortwave transmitters at Daventry in Northamptonshire. In order to ensure the greatest sense of imperial unity, it was felt the speech should be broadcast simultaneously across all of the empire, and would be preceded by an hour-long programme of greetings from the empire's furthest reaches. This required careful scheduling to ensure the largest possible audience, and the most favourable broadcasting conditions for the notoriously fickle shortwave transmission. The time chosen was 3 p.m. Greenwich Mean Time; prime evening listening in New Delhi and Colombo (8.30 p.m.) and mid-morning for 'white settlers' listening in Canada and the Caribbean. Listeners in Australia and New Zealand got a particularly raw deal, with the broadcast crackling out noisily from radio sets in Sydney and Auckland on Boxing Day morning, at 2 a.m. and 4 a.m. respectively. The lateness of the hour, and the missing of the day, didn't seem to dampen the enthusiasm of those listening down under, at least not in those listeners who wrote to the BBC in the weeks and months that followed the broadcast. *World Radio* published one such letter from a correspondent in Australia:

The Christmas Day programme sent a thrill of pride through every Australian. Australians are particularly loyal to the Empire as an Institution, and the thing that stirred us most was the roll-call. As the announcer went round the Empire, following the setting sun, we went with him.[11]

Radio appeared to have the power to 'move', emotionally, but also to metaphorically transport and mobilize the imaginations of listeners on a sonic grand tour of the empire. The *Daily Telegraph* described the event in similar terms: 'thrilling', 'moving', 'affecting' – and not only of emotions or imaginations but also of bodies. 'How many family circles acted, I wonder, as the one did of which I heard yesterday', the newspaper asked rhetorically. 'Without a word, and with eyes here and there filling with tears, they rose and joined in the National Anthem with the BBC orchestra.'[12]

As the historian Simon Potter has noted, claims made to the affective and emotional appeal of the Empire Service and its peculiar ability to unite far-flung peoples into some semblance of an 'on air' community anticipated some of the key claims made by the influential Canadian media theorist Marshall McLuhan by nearly thirty years.[13] Today McLuhan is often best remembered for his concepts of 'hot' and 'cold' media (radio was deemed to be hot), his dictum that 'the medium is the message', and his walk-on cameo appearance in Woody Allen's romantic comedy *Annie Hall* (1977), but it was 'space' and spatial inequalities that represented the single most consistent conceptual category running through his scholarship.[14] As well as developing the concept of 'the global village' and 'visual' and 'acoustic' spaces, McLuhan considered radio to be the revival of 'the tribal drum' and 'the kit of the global villager' in recognition that it had the capability to 'contract the world to village size and creates village tastes for gossip, rumor and personal malice'. McLuhan also recognized that radio was productive of new and alternative kinds of places and spatial experiences (including, as we have already seen, *Lebensraums*) and capable of reviving 'the ancient experience of kinship webs'.[15] Although writing in the 1960s, the concepts McLuhan was developing seem to have been understood within the 1930s Empire Service, not least as it became apparent that the BBC's broadcasting schedules informed new habits, routines and rhythms of British, empire and commonwealth life. One fairly widely reported phenomenon involved Empire Service audiences synchronizing their timepieces to correspond with the broadcast chimes of Big Ben despite being physically located in Burma or remote villages in India and multiple time zones removed from Greenwich. In a similar way, the earliest transmission requirements of the Empire Service continue to reverberate through Britain and the modern Commonwealth, most obviously through the continued observance of 3 o'clock as the moment on Christmas Day when the Monarch's Christmas Day message is broadcast via radio and television.

THE KING'S SPEECH

For all his initial reluctance, King George V proved to be a natural broadcaster with considerable vocal gravitas. His Christmas 1932 speech – scripted by the renowned journalist, novelist and 'poet of the empire', Rudyard Kipling – captured the imagination of listeners, but the speech was just as important as a carrier wave for the king's own voice, which was noted for its gravelly quality and seemed to confirm, orally and aurally, George V as the benevolent patriarch of the empire. 'Untold thousands of people must have been hearing the King's voice for the first time,' speculated the *Daily Telegraph*. 'Everyone that I spoke to had been greatly impressed by its virile vigour, but what affected them most was the note of fatherly affection which rang through every word of the historic utterance.' His words ran:

> Through one of the marvels of modern Science, I am enabled, this Christmas Day, to speak to all my peoples throughout the Empire. I take it as a good omen that Wireless should have reached its

present perfection at a time when the Empire has been linked in closer union. For it offers us immense possibilities to make that union closer still. It may be that our future may lay upon us more than one stern test. Our past will have taught us how to meet it unshaken. For the present, the work to which we are all equally bound is to arrive at a reasoned tranquillity within our borders; to regain prosperity without self-seeking; and to carry with us those whom the burden of past years has disheartened or overborne. My life's aim has been to serve as I might, towards those ends. Your loyalty, your confidence in me has been my abundant reward.

I speak now from my home and from my heart to you all. To men and women so cut off by the snows, the desert or the sea, that only voices out of the air can reach them; to those cut off from fuller life by blindness, sickness, or infirmity; and to those who are celebrating this day with their children and grand-children. To all – to each – I wish a Happy Christmas. God Bless You![16]

For many, the speech and the distant strains of Big Ben that had preceded it offered both a nostalgic reminder of home and a feeling of being 'at home'. Kipling's words had purposefully evoked a kind of imagined community 'of the air' that acoustically bound individuals – and even more obviously, households – into the mutual endeavours of empire. The act of listening to the Empire Service gradually became, in itself, a means for listeners to realize a connection with the wider empire. Even in the Dominions, the Empire Service served to maintain a shared sense of 'Britishness' at a time when distinctly 'national' identities (and independence movements) were emerging. Radio listening had both a performative and visual dimension. In order to receive Empire broadcasts, listeners required radio sets capable of receiving shortwave broadcasts and erect aerials with the capacity to pick out of the airborne shortwave signals travelling thousands of kilometres from their starting point on a hill above Daventry in central England. Aerial arrays throughout the empire needed to be physically orientated deferentially towards

the United Kingdom for the best hope of radio reception. The BBC published a range of practical maps, depicting 'lines of broadcast' and geographical bearings, to help their listeners' electromagnetic homage to London. This new imperial centrality was further emphasized in the BBC's official Christmas card from 1936, drawn by Macdonald Gill who updated his previous 'sea routes of empire' maps to visually illustrate Britain's new electromagnetic trading routes.

BBC postcard to the empire, December 1936.

For listeners in colonial possessions elsewhere around the empire, the BBC Empire Service (renamed Overseas Service in 1939) was heard with rather more ambivalence than in the so-called 'White Dominions'. In India, where support for full independence from Britain had fermented since the end of the First World War, the Empire Service sounded rather less like the strains of 'home', the 'mother country' or an 'ever closer union' than the voice of an increasingly unwelcome colonial master. This was especially the case after the outbreak of war in 1939, when BBC broadcasts encouraged subjected peoples to rise up against their oppressors in occupied Europe, while asking Indians to remain loyal – an irony that was all too obvious to newspaper cartoonists at the time. Further injurious broadcasts would follow. Indian listeners reported an 'insult to Asiatic people' when they overheard a speech on the BBC's Australia/New Zealand transmission (which was entirely audible in India) by the Australian prime minister, in which he proclaimed: 'We are fighting to obtain a white Australia.' The broadcasts were later reused within Japanese propaganda, and reportedly had a 'direct effect on our Indian troops'. Other incidents involved ill-judged reference to the Black Hole of Calcutta and the 'absurd mispronunciation' of India place names. As one colonial official noted, 'Peshawar, Rawalpindi, Deccan, Deolali, Mhow, Delhi, all wrong. This creates a bad impression here.' Some months later, the same official felt it necessary to telegram London again. 'Good effect of publicity being given by BBC to exploits of Indian troops in Africa is somewhat marred by mistakes in announcing,' he reported. 'For instance two occurred in 9.30 IST [India Standard Time], news bulletin on 6th March. The first syllable of Punjab rhymes with "gun" and "Dogra" is not name of place in Africa but of an Indian martial tribe. Can you convey this delicately to BBC?'[17] By the end of the war in 1945, the mistakes that dogged the BBC's earlier broadcasts had been largely addressed, and the service was audible across the subcontinent in Hindi (1940), Burmese (1940), Tamil (1941), Bengali (1941), Gujarati (1942), Sinhala (1942) and Marathi (1944). For many employees, the BBC's broadcasts to India posed a moral dilemma. For the likes of Eric Blair, who supervised the production of cultural programming on the Indian-language services from 1941 until 1943, it was a case of 'defending the bad against the worse', the Raj against the Reich.[18] Blair is, today, better remembered by his nom de plume, George Orwell, and as the author of *Animal Farm* (1945) and *1984* (1949), both of which draw on Orwell's wartime experiences working for the BBC's overseas services. The now infamous Room 101

– the site of state torture in *1984* – was inspired by a conference room (and the tedious meetings that took place within it) at Broadcasting House. Orwell is now commemorated in bronze outside the same building in central London. Accompanying the statue are the words from the original preface to *Animal Farm*: 'If liberty means anything at all, it means the right to tell people what they do not want to hear.' Shortwave broadcasting would ensure that 'right' had global dimensions, and global consequences.

CHALLENGING AND REGULATING INTERNATIONAL AIR

'Internal' broadcasting – the practice of broadcasting solely to the domestic population of a particular nation state – has long been considered a practical impossibility within Europe. The intensity and proximity of international frontiers meant that the transnational bleeding of wireless transmissions from one country to another was (and remains) a commonplace occurrence. By the 1930s, the intensity of radio activity within and between Europe's political frontiers had prompted both the beginnings of a 'radio war' and growing calls for a new kind of international regime to regulate wireless transmissions.

In 1926, the total power output of European broadcasting systems was estimated to measure 116 kilowatts. By 1938, that power output had grown to 8,000 kilowatts. Conventional broadcasting wisdom suggests that increased transmitter power translates into stronger radio signals and improved audibility for audiences. However, in the context of Europe in the 1930s, increased power really translated into the expanded geographical range of transmitter stations and a heightened competition for listeners across international borders. In one such example from Eastern Europe, the power of the transmitter in Prague was increased in order to challenge Hungarian broadcasts transgressing the Czech-Hungarian international border. Hungarian transmitter power was, in turn, increased for the stated purpose of adequately reaching Hungarian-speaking populations inside Czechoslovakia and Yugoslavia. In an environment where there seemed to be 'no frontiers in the air', Yugoslavia reacted by building a new transmitter station in order to communicate with Slavs at home and abroad and to 'drown out Hungarian revisionist propaganda'.[19] Elsewhere, Nazi Germany jammed German-language transmissions from Strasbourg (for the peoples of Alsace) after they were heard deep into German territory, while simultaneously deploying powerful transmitters in order to promote German influence throughout Czechoslovakia, Poland, Lithuania, Latvia, Romania and Yugoslavia: an acoustic *Lebensraum*. Writing in 1938, the American media observer César Saerchinger noted that

> The European propaganda machines seem to have been perfected. The voices of the national stentors are now so loud that the ordinary listener to international programs often finds his pleasure spoiled by competing political broadcasts.[20]

It is an undoubtedly curious state of perfection in which the 'loudness' of broadcasts is given primacy over the capacity of the audience to hear them. Nonetheless, Saerchinger noted an even more sinister aspect to this emergent radio war. Increased transmitter power and improvements in broadcast technology had added to the cacophony of radio signals within Europe, but it also allowed the burgeoning radio war to spill beyond the continental boundaries of Europe altogether. Italy was at the forefront of this extra-regional escalation. Beginning in 1934, Mussolini's fascist government had requisitioned the transmitters of Radio Bari, a provincial transmitting station in the Apulia region of southern Italy, for the purposes of exporting Italy's own brand of international propaganda. Directed outwards, across the Mediterranean, towards North Africa and the Middle East, Bari's transmitters carried broadcasts in Arabic towards Libya (an Italian colony) and coastal regions of Egypt, Palestine, Syria, Algeria and Morocco. Shortwave transmitters in Rome relayed the broadcasts still further into areas of particular British influence around the Suez Canal and the Red Sea. The transmissions delivered a rich diet of cultural propaganda glorifying the achievements of Italy and the fascist regime with the stated aim being to 'strengthen ties between Italy and the Arab peoples'. Underlying this somewhat innocuous ambition lay rather more strategic imperatives. First, there was a recognized need for Italy to rehabilitate its reputation in the Arab world following the tarnish of Italian atrocities committed during the so-called 'pacification of Libya'. Radio, it was hoped, might prove somehow redemptive, cleansing. In this vein, the Bari transmissions heralded Mussolini as the 'protector of Islam', a title which was more formally (but no less problematically) bestowed upon him during a visit to Tripoli in 1937. The broadcasts, often presented as 'news' and 'news commentaries', also sought to challenge British and French influence in the region, and did so by deploying an increasingly aggressive and violent form of broadcasting designed to 'whip up Arab nationalism' in the years after 1935.[21] British and French policies in the region were routinely attacked 'in the most extreme terms' with the hope that strategic resources (and the limited supply of Anglo- and Franco-Arab goodwill) would be consumed in quelling any subsequent unrest.

Crucial to, and underpinning, this strategy of subversion and disruption was the medium of radio itself. It was mobile enough as a technology to be capable of travelling throughout Arabic-speaking North Africa and the Middle East from fixed points deep within the Italian homeland. In a region of high illiteracy, its oral message could break through barriers of understanding and comprehension in a way that newspapers and pamphlets could not. The personal ownership of radios in the Middle East region was also on the rise during the late 1920s and early 1930s. The British authorities in Palestine issued 10,000 radio licences during 1935, although this statistic fails to account for additional audiences through shared or communal listening. Radio's ability to speak to multiple listeners at the same moment via integrated or auxiliary loudspeakers not only increased its reach but intensified contact with its audience. By the mid-1930s Arab café owners in Egypt and Palestine had become fond of installing wireless receivers in their premises for the entertainment of patrons. Within the intensely convivial atmosphere of the café, distant voices were brought close, listened to, discussed, debated and lent greater authority through this kind of *active* consumption of 'the wireless'. Notwithstanding some initial missteps in Radio Bari's inception, including the use of Libyan announcers who spoke in the 'strangulated' tones of classical Arabic (and were reportedly subject to ridicule by listeners), the station's careful blend of news, propaganda and musical entertainment quickly gained a loyal following both at home and in the cafés, where it was reported Arab customers 'sipped their coffee and swallowed Italian propaganda with every mouthful'. In a vivid, if somewhat orientalist, description, the journalist, media observer and former British Information Service operative Charles Rolo (1916–1982) noted that long-established traditions of coffee drinking

Yemenite rabbi listening in the radio in British Mandatory Palestine, 1930s.

and political conversation were further enlivened by the disembodied voices emanating from café loudspeakers:

> When the day's work was done both the *fellaheen* (peasants) and the city dwellers would betake themselves to their favourite cafes, huddle together under a fuming oil lamp, and stolidly smoking their water pipes play game after game of backgammon until the communal loudspeakers gave forth to the Bari announcer.[22]

In French-controlled Algeria, a similar pattern of collective listening was reported within *le café maure* (Moorish tea houses), *cercles* (Muslim associations) and even brothels; in fact anywhere Algerian men might gather, collectively, to listen to the radio.[23] In areas of both French and British influence there was uncertainty about the most effective means of responding to the challenge of international broadcasting. Decision-making was undoubtedly made all the more difficult by rumoured reports that Italian agents had taken to selling, in large quantities, 'cheap radios to the Arabs, capable of receiving only Italian broadcasts'.[24] Although no evidence was ever received to confirm these rumours, the real and imagined effects of Italy's inflammatory broadcasting had certainly provoked consternation and even a hint of panic in London and Paris. Senior commanders of British Forces in Palestine and Trans-Jordan suggested jamming Bari's broadcasts using naval vessels positioned in the Mediterranean, 80 km (50 mi.) off the coast, making it difficult for the Italian government to trace the source of the jamming. British lawmakers and strategists in London were, perhaps inevitably, more cautious in their proposals. Fearing an escalation of tensions with Italy and further electromagnetic reprisals (such as the intensification of Italian propaganda in the Middle East and even the interference with British naval and maritime communications), the British government advocated a diplomatic solution to radio's international challenge.

The eventual outcome of these diplomatic efforts, coordinated in order to de-escalate initial forays into international propaganda broadcasting, was an agreement by the inter-war League of Nations to a multilateral treaty prohibiting the use of broadcasting for propaganda or the spreading of false news. The 'International Convention concerning the Use of Broadcasting in the Cause of Peace' (1936) was a remarkably progressive attempt to limit interference in the sovereign affairs of another state via broadcasting and the first international treaty of its kind to compel states to cease broadcasts that might constitute a threat to international peace and security. The United Kingdom (including all imperial possessions and territories) ratified the treaty in 1937 (only officially renouncing it in 1985), but it was a treaty that was, in reality, doomed to failure from the outset. Germany, Italy and Japan refused to sign or ratify the treaty and pursued aggressive international propaganda unabated.

TROJAN RADIO

The Cold War was arguably the high-water mark in radio's particular 'globalization'. In the absence of direct military conflict, radio emerged as a crucial technological proxy (alongside cinema, literature and other forums such as the Olympic Games) in what Frances Stonor Saunders has called the 'cultural Cold War'.[25] National governments aligned to both the United States and the Soviet Union channelled enormous financial and technological resources into the science and practice of international radio broadcasting, while the availability of affordable radio sets enlarged radio audiences to unprecedented levels in the Soviet bloc, Europe, North America and emerging developing countries.

Radio and its potential effect on the minds of citizens was the source of frequent moral panic within the United States, in particular. Speaking in Denver in 1950, General Dwight D. Eisenhower (1890–1969) warned of the electromagnetic threat posed by

powerful Communist radio stations [that] incessantly tell the world that we Americans are physically soft and morally corrupt; that we

Promoting Radio
Free Europe, which
received CIA funding
from 1951 to 1972.

are disunited and confused; that we are selfish and cowardly;
that we have nothing to offer the world but imperialism and
exploitation.[26]

In response and retaliation, Eisenhower backed calls for the United
States to 'counteract the Communist deceits' through new investment
in 'powerful radio stations abroad, operated without government
restriction'.[27] Eisenhower's 'Campaign for Freedom' became a major
supporter and fundraiser for Radio Free Europe (which targeted the
Soviet satellite states) and Radio Liberty (which targeted the Soviet
Union), both of which were later exposed as CIA-financed operations.

A perennial challenge for U.S. radio stations seeking to 'perforate'
the Iron Curtain was the Soviet development of jamming technologies.
By September 1949, the Soviet Union had invested somewhere in the
region of $70 million in 250 sky-wave transmitters and five hundred
ground-wave transmitters, and were blocking up to 90 per cent of
Western transmissions, with an annual operating cost of $17 million
per year. By comparison, the total annual operating budget of the BBC
Overseas Services in 1949 was £5.35 million. In order to overcome the
effects of Soviet jamming, the U.S. Department of Defense invested in
new, experimental, 'blue sky' and highly classified 'political warfare'
projects, led by interdisciplinary scientists from MIT, Harvard and other
leading universities. In the spirit of the age, a range of more and less practical propositions were considered – from the use of high-power beam

antennae, located near the borders of the Soviet Union, that could be swung round in the hope of overwhelming and circumventing the effect of jamming stations, to the use of the Moon as a giant radio-reflector in order to bypass Soviet jamming altogether. In the end, the appropriately named 'Project Troy' proposed two more practical options: first the use of weather balloons to drop pre-tuned radio sets deep inside Soviet territory; and, second, the development of a new suite of high-power broadcasting facilities in strategic sites encircling the Soviet Union – ranging from Alaska to Germany, Greece, Ceylon (now Sri Lanka), Thailand, the Philippines and Japan. This would be further augmented by the use of ship-mounted transmitters where necessary. Known as the 'Ring Plan' for obvious reasons, the scheme was adopted as the blueprint for the expansion of the U.S.-government controlled Voice of America (VOA) radio station, although it was a scheme that was never fully realized. Despite receiving political and financial support from

Radio transmitters designated for use by Voice of America (1940s–60s) at the u.s. naval base at Pearl Harbor.

Senator Joseph
McCarthy, June 1954.

the u.s. Congress, cost overruns and political interference in siting the
u.s.-based transmitters played a part in thwarting the effort. The Ring
Plan would ultimately be finished off by the anti-communist witch-
hunts led by Senator Joseph McCarthy. Beginning in 1953, McCarthy
claimed that VOA was riddled with 'left-wingers' and 'pro-reds' and that
the broadcaster as a whole was insufficiently fervent in its promotion
of American values overseas. Under McCarthy's chairmanship, the
investigations of the Committee on Government Operations ensured
that funding for the Ring Plan was cut off, and maximum damage was
done – operationally and reputationally – to one of the Cold War's
most important international broadcasting stations.

5
RADIO WARS

Running in parallel with utopian visions for the democratic communion of humankind 'in the ether' have been darker and more sinister visions for radio – as a strategic device to grab power, secure resources, quell uprisings, deploy military assets and to threaten and persuade. In short, visions of radio as a weapon of war par excellence. Writing in 1924, the noted physicist, inventor and author Archibald Low (1888–1956) mused that 'the subjects of War and Wireless cover a multitude of closely allied ills.' Low foresaw radio's widespread application in: making warfare more efficient; assisting in targeted aerial bombing and the detection of sub-surface objects (what we now call ground-penetrating radar); the encryption of radio communications (such that 'correspondence can be undertaken with a reasonable degree of secrecy'); the networked battlefield, where we will see 'whole armies in instantaneous touch with one another'; and what we would now call Unmanned Aerial Vehicles (UAVs).[1] As Low said:

> The time will come when low-flying wireless planes will explore, and render visible at many miles distant, places where no human pilot could remain for any length of time in safety.[2]

The rapid adoption of UAVs, or drones, for counterterrorism operations 'on . . . land, air and water', seem particularly prescient. 'All will be accurately controlled,' he anticipated, 'and they will possibly be able to

find their way home and to operate from a distance while out of sight.' The IDF's new vehicles are reported to be controlled by operators who can be hidden up to 3 km (nearly 2 mi.) away. Some of Low's other predictions have not yet come to fruition, although they have been subject to considerable and ongoing speculation, including the 'electric death ray' and radio-based weapons that are able to harvest thoughts and ideas directly from the human mind.[3]

Low's pamphlet was not altogether a work of speculation. During the First World War, Low had been the head of Experimental Works in the Royal Flying Corps (the precursor to the RAF) and had overseen the highly secretive development of radio-controlled, pilotless aeroplanes. Purposefully misnamed the 'Aerial Target' (AT) to confuse German spies, the AT programme was, in reality, designed to provide the UK with aerial defences against German Zeppelins and flying bombs. While the AT project lost support immediately after the armistice, Low's technologies lived on through Britain's experimental Larynx anti-ship weapon programme (1925–9) – said to be one of the first 'cruise' missile systems – and as a source of inspiration for German weapons engineers involved in the highly secretive *Kirschkern* (Cherrystone) weapons project.[4]

Cherrystone culminated in the Vergeltungswaffe-1 (or V-1) flying bomb, also known as the doodlebug because of the characteristic buzzing sound of its pulsejet engine. Twelve thousand V-1s were launched towards southeast England and Antwerp during the latter years of the war.

RADIO'S WAR WITH THE HUMAN MIND

> Thousands of terror-stricken radio listeners throughout the country fled from their homes last night when they tuned in on a series of synthetic news broadcasts which depicted the beginning of an interplanetary war.[5]

Newspaper reports filled American newspaper pages in the days following the now-infamous broadcast of H. G. Wells's 1898 novel *The War of the Worlds* in October 1938. The programme, broadcast on America's Columbia Broadcasting System (CBS) radio network, was found so realistic in its styling and delivery by its audience that it sent a wave of mass hysteria across the continent. Apartment blocks are said to have emptied as first-hand listeners responded to the supposed threat and then multiplied the impeding peril by warning their friends and neighbours. One woman in Pittsburgh, according to newspaper reports, attempted suicide. Another was badly injured in her rush to escape her home. Citizens of New York hastily took to their cars in order to escape the impending 'bombing' of the city. Others reportedly participated in mass prayer sessions in order to seek salvation. *The War of the Worlds* was, of course, a work of fiction. There was no such invasion, although the drama did certainly unfold through a series of fictionalized news broadcasts that were presented without the interruption of adverts (unusual on U.S. radio at the time) for at least the first thirty minutes of the transmission. The programme's director, Orson Welles (1915–1985), speculated in the hours that followed that, perhaps, radio itself had contributed to the mass deception:

We can only suppose that the special nature of radio, which is often heard in fragments, or in parts disconnected from the whole, has led to this misunderstanding.[6]

While the true extent of the 'hysteria' over *The War of the Worlds* broadcast was, almost certainly, massively overstated (and itself something of a fiction), there was certainly no doubt that radio's power to inform and potential to persuade had become the subject of national (and international) speculation, intrigue and even fear.

What effect could radio have on populations listening within the confines of their own homes? How would listening to the human voice delivering news and information differ from that of the written word? These questions, as we have seen, were born out of emergent moral anxieties about the effect of local and national radio on listeners during the late 1920s and 1930s. Radio, it was widely believed, had a role to play in the development of 'the nation', but the kind of radio nation that would emerge would depend on the stimuli carried to listeners over the air. By the mid- to late 1930s these domestic moral anxieties were increasingly becoming strategic imperatives on an international scale. At almost precisely the same time that the BBC Empire Service was extending its reach throughout the 'Pax Britannica' and George V was learning to embrace radio's imperial opportunities, experiments were underway in the United States that sought to reveal something of the psychology of radio. Working out of laboratories at Harvard University, two experimental social psychologists, Gordon Allport (1897–1967) and Hadley Cantril (1906–1969), were seeking 'to map out . . . the new mental world created by radio' – exploring the effects that radio had on its audiences and the ways in which listeners related to, and made sense of, radio's broadcasting codes, conventions and voices.[7] It is worth mentioning two experiments in particular. The first experiment involved more than six hundred participants, who were asked to listen to a range of male voices broadcast through loudspeakers into the Harvard psychology laboratory and to note their instinctive reactions to those voices. Cantril and Allport were particularly interested to discover whether the participants were inclined, or indeed able, to determine physical ('outer') characteristics or personality-linked ('inner') traits of the various speakers. Could listeners accurately determine features such as the age, height, appearance or political preference of complete strangers solely through the broadcast of the human voice? The results, it would be fair to say, were a bit of a mixed bag. No single human characteristic – outer or inner – was always identified accurately by listeners, although on average their judgements were considered 'more accurate' than would be expected by chance. Nonetheless, the experiment did reveal something more certain: that listeners to radio invested the voices they heard with distinct personalities and, moreover, that the disembodied voices appeared to conjure up mental images of the speaker in the imagination – or 'mind's eye' – of the listener.

In a second experiment, participants were divided into two groups, one of which was asked to read a printed script while the other listened to the script read out over loudspeakers. The results of this experiment were arguably even more extraordinary than those of the 'voice-personality' experiment. It was found that the group who listened to the script were much less critical recipients of the information they heard than those who had read the same information. Listeners were much more likely to believe what they had heard over the loudspeaker and were less questioning and more 'well disposed' towards the information being broadcast.[8] These, and other experiments written up in Allport and Cantril's foundational work, led the researchers to several important conclusions about radio. 'Without doubt,' they claimed, 'radio is a more sociable means of communication than the written word. What is spoken is fluid, alive, contemporary; it belongs in a personal context . . . the human voice is more interesting, more persuasive, more friendly, and more compelling than is the written word.'[9] Radio broadcasting seemed, almost, to possess special powers. The broadcast voice – disembodied and unfamiliar to listeners – was treated as a real (or imagined) *person*, speaking *personally* to individual listeners, building up bonds of trust, even friendship, and with a facility to persuade or influence. But if radio had the capacity to forge intense personal relationships with individual listeners, it could also build feelings of membership – a 'consciousness of kind' as Allport and Cantril describe it – between individual listeners, even those physically separated by great distances, class, ethnicity, gender and so on.[10]

The act of listening simultaneously might, in other words, lead to the creation of 'a crowd mind' or, as Benedict Anderson would later call it, a sense of being in an 'imagined community'.[11] Taken together, these capabilities seemed astonishing and contributed to a sense that radio was mysterious, even uncanny; not only able to penetrate walls and enter the home, but somehow able to enter the mind in new and unanticipated ways.

Russian villagers listen in to the state loudspeaker, 1932.

Published in 1935, this research and its conclusions did not shy away from addressing the commercial, political and even geopolitical agencies that were influencing the development of radio within the United States and wider international arena at the time. Allport and Cantril's anxieties about radio's futures infuse their work. In a startlingly outspoken set of recommendations, the two researchers called for radio in the United States to be 'kept free from narrow political domination' and proposed safeguarding it from 'the dictatorship of private profits'. On an international scale, they feared an even more sinister form of dictatorship:

> Most of us have already heard the sound of a bell striking the hour in Westminster, and a voice issuing out of the fastness of the Antarctic. We realize that the day cannot be far off when men in every country of the globe will be able to listen at one time to the persuasions or commands of some wizard seated in a central palace of broadcasting, possessed of a power more fantastic than that of Aladdin.[12]

By the time that Allport and Cantril were making their assessments, the rise of authoritarian regimes was already well underway in Europe, with radio in technological support. Beginning in Russia, Italy and latterly Germany, radio broadcasting was not only implicated in the 'service of the state', it was also an essential electromagnetic conduit through which political authority was realized, practised and enforced. In Soviet Russia, the number of state-owned radio transmitters increased from four to fifty between 1926 and 1928 as Lenin sought to bring the expanse of the Soviet Union within earshot of Moscow. Comrades would have little option but to listen to the voice of the state via loudspeakers that were erected in schools, factories and even apartment buildings. As we have seen, the Nazis pursued a similar policy following their rise to power in 1933, enabled by the development of the affordable 'People's Receiver'. In Italy, Benito Mussolini – *Il Duce* – exerted personal control over the Italian airwaves from the mid-1920s, slowly moving the Ente Italiano per le Audizioni Radiofoniche (EIAR), the Italian national broadcaster, under the direct influence of his Ministry of Press and Propaganda.

Just as Europe's authoritarian regimes sought to exert control over *their* air, so they also contributed to an increasingly turbulent

broadcasting atmosphere across the continent. By the mid-1930s Europe was blanketed by electromagnetic signals and wireless broadcasts that resisted Westphalian notions of the state and refused to observe the diplomatic niceties usually required at international political boundaries. Radio's influence was being felt everywhere: travelling silently through space, traversing international frontiers with seeming impunity, and increasingly implicated in assertive and even aggressive European border politics. Radio seemed less like the voice of a friend, and more that of a troublesome neighbour.

Mapping radio ownership in wartime Germany by the U.S. Office for Strategic Service (OSS), the forerunner of the CIA (1941).

Monitoring foreign radio broadcasts at the BBC during the Second World War, c. 1940.

HATE AND HATEFUL RADIO

Radio's capacities to inspire anxiety, fear and a range of emotional responses, including hatred, have been well known and eagerly pursued since the 1930s, when the Nazi propaganda machine was deployed to inspire loathing of European Jews. This was not a solely German phenomenon, nor one confined to the period of radio's comparative infancy.

In the United States, Father Charles Coughlin (1891–1971), an ordained Roman Catholic priest, had become a familiar and powerful radio voice during the late 1920s and 1930s. Dubbed the 'Radio Priest', it is estimated that almost one-third of all radio listeners in the U.S. – perhaps 40 million people per week – would tune in to Coughlin's particular blend of religiously infused political commentary. Initially a supporter of Franklin D. Roosevelt's presidency, he later turned against FDR following the introduction of the New Deal programme. And yet, Coughlin was also damning of the financial practices of American corporate giants (such as Standard Oil), a powerful advocate for the unionization of the labour force, and a vocal critic of both communism and Nazism. Nonetheless, by the mid-1930s, Coughlin's broadcasts had taken on a distinctly discomfiting tone as he enrolled so-called 'Jewish conspirators' into his panoply of evil-doers. When Coughlin took to the airwaves on 20 November 1938, just two weeks after Kristallnacht, a pogrom of ransacking that targeted Jewish shops, homes and synagogues, and announced that 'Jewish persecution only followed after Christians first were persecuted', radio stations across the United States dropped Coughlin's 'The Hour of Power' radio programme from their schedules, sparking in some cases large and vocal demonstrations but also dramatically reducing his reach and influence. The outbreak of the Second World War in 1939 and the introduction of tighter broadcasting regulations finally forced radio stations to remove Coughlin from the airwaves altogether in 1940. Despite his shortened radio career, Coughlin's broadcasts galvanized anti-Semitism in the U.S.

Father Charles
Coughlin, the 'Radio
Priest' of the Great
Depression.

and continue to resonate within U.S. political culture as a longer-term
warning to broadcasters and politicians about the power of charismatic
speakers, possessed of commanding 'radio voices', to assert political
influence 'over the air'. Coughlin has been labelled as 'the father'
and 'the pioneer' of 'hate radio'. Since the liberalization of the U.S.
airwaves in the 1980s under President Reagan with the repeal of the
so-called 'balance laws', U.S. radio has again become a space of political controversy thanks to the emergence of a new breed of politicized
broadcasters, including Rush Limbaugh and Glenn Beck.

    If hate radio was pioneered by Coughlin during the 1930s, it
arguably reached its unwelcome maturity during the 1990s as a sonic
accompaniment to the civil fracturing of the Balkans and, more in-
famously, the country of Rwanda. The most notorious hate radio
stations were Radio Rwanda (the official state radio station of the
Rwandan government) and Radio Télévision Libre des Milles Collines
(RTLM). Even before the Rwandan genocide (April–July 1994), these
stations preyed upon the fears and anxieties of Rwanda's Hutu-majority

community by broadcasting a relentless denigration of ethnic Tutsis, Belgians, the United Nations' mission in Rwanda, and even moderate Hutus. But it was the Tutsi ethnic minority population that was the primary focus of RTLM's campaign of hatred. *Inyenzi* (cockroaches) became a regularly used on-air code word for Tutsis, and wild accusations filled the airwaves about alleged spying, corruption and sinister plots to enslave Hutus. RTLM called for a 'final war' to hasten their extermination, broadcast daily lists of known Tutsis and their geographical locations, and vocally encouraged bands of heavily armed *Interahamwe* paramilitaries who were scouring the country to 'go to work'.[13] Subsequent reports have suggested that RTLM broadcasts directly contributed to over 50,000 deaths during the Rwandan genocide between 1993 and 1994. The International Criminal Tribunal for Rwanda (ICTR, 1995–2015), convened in the northern Tanzanian city of Arusha, ultimately determined that RTLM and Radio Rwanda had played a crucial role in fermenting an atmosphere of racial hostility that allowed the genocide to occur. In 2003, the tribunal found Ferdinand Nahimana (b. 1950) and Jean-Bosco Barayagwiza, RTLM's executives, guilty on charges of genocide, incitement to genocide and crimes against humanity, before and during the period of the genocides of 1994. They were sentenced to be imprisoned for thirty years and 32 years respectively. In 2009, one of the most notorious RTLM announcers, Valérie Bemeriki (b. 1955), was convicted by a Rwandan court and sentenced to life imprisonment for her role in inciting genocidal atrocities. In one broadcast attributed to Bemeriki, she announced: 'Do not kill those cockroaches with a bullet – cut them to pieces with a machete.' In giving their verdicts, the ICTR judges reflected on radio's particular spoken and unspoken registers, and affective capacities:

> RTLM broadcasting was a drumbeat, calling on listeners to take action against the enemy and enemy accomplices, equated with the Tutsi population. The phrase 'heating up heads' captures the process of incitement systematically engaged in by RTLM, which

after 6 April 1994 was also known as 'Radio Machete'. The nature of radio transmission made RTLM particularly dangerous and harmful, as did the breadth of its reach. Unlike print media, radio is immediately present and active. The power of the human voice, heard by the Chamber when the broadcast tapes were played in Kinyarwanda, adds a quality and dimension beyond words to the message conveyed. In this setting, radio heightened the sense of fear, the sense of danger and the sense of urgency giving rise to the need for action by listeners. The denigration of Tutsi ethnicity was augmented by the visceral scorn coming out of the airwaves – the ridiculing laugh and the nasty sneer. These elements greatly amplified the impact of RTLM broadcasts.[14]

In giving their verdicts, the ICTR took into account radio's peculiar immediacy and agency, as well as the taut and intimate relationship between listener and broadcaster. In short, they reflected radio's dramatic potential. More recently, novelists, playwrights and film-makers have responded to radio's inculcation in the systemic violence of the Rwandan genocide. Dramatized RTLM broadcasts were used throughout the film *Hotel Rwanda* (2004, dir. Terry George), while *Shooting Dogs/Beyond the Gates* (2005, dir. Michael Caton-Jones) intersperses real RTLM recordings in a powerful critique of the futility of the UN mission. In *Sometimes in April* (2005, dir. Raoul Peck), we are introduced to the protagonist's brother, Honoré, seated in the dock during the ICTR tribunals in 2004, before cutting to a scene some ten years earlier in the studios of RTLM, where we see him – and hear him – delivering anti-Tutsi denunciations, despite his sister-in-law, nephews and nieces being classified as ethnically Tutsi. On the theatre's stage, *Hate Radio* (2011, dir. Milo Rau) reproduces with extraordinary accuracy the RTLM studios in Kigali as a space in which issues of racism and ethnic 'othering' can be explored through dramatic reconstructions of notorious RTLM broadcasts and corresponding witness statements.

RADIO'S WAR WITH THE MATERIAL WORLD

From the earliest moments of radio experimentation, it was recognized that material objects – whether mobile or static – had the capacity to interfere with the clear reception of radio signals over distance. Radio pioneers, including Marconi, who were locked in a struggle for improved clarity and greater transmission distance for wireless telegraphy, sought to reduce the effects of such interference through incremental improvements to the design and power of their apparatus – and, of course, by elevating their apparatus high above the ground in order to reduce interference from the largest material object of all, the Earth itself. Interference was inconvenient for those motivated by extending radio's range. Others, however, had started to see potential in radio's 'interaction' with the material world. During experimental ship-to-ship communications in the Baltic Sea in 1897, for example, Alexander Popov (1859–1906), a physics instructor at the Imperial Russian Navy College, observed a distinct pattern of interference caused by the movements of a ship, which led him to speculate whether radio might be specifically applied in the detection of objects. Not untypically in the somewhat fragmented history of radio, Popov didn't pursue this particular observation, although the baton was taken up in Germany by another physicist, Christian Hülsmeyer (1881–1957), who demonstrated his experimental equipment in the rather more genteel surroundings of the central courtyard of the Dom Hotel in Cologne in 1904. Hülsmeyer's so-called 'Telemobiloscope' caught the public imagination by detecting the presence of the hotel's impressive gothic metal gates even when they were obscured from sight by a set of drawn curtains. Subsequent 'sea trials' of the Telemobiloscope produced more mixed results. Although Hülsmeyer showed that he could detect the presence of shipping within a 3.2-km (2-mi.) radius, even in thick fog, the equipment wasn't capable of determining the range/distance of the objects being detected. Patents were subsequently overturned and rejected for non-payment of fees, and the company was dissolved shortly thereafter. Despite this faltering start, Popov and Hülsmeyer had demonstrated the feasibility of radio detection, although it would take another twenty years for the theory and apparatus to advance to the point of full operability.

By the mid-1930s, experiments into radio's capacity to detect and locate objects had a renewed impetus and were rather less focused on the watery environment of the seas, and rather more concerned with the presence of objects in the skies. With geopolitical tensions in Europe slowly increasing, lingering memories of Zeppelin raids over London during the First World War, and airfields in continental Europe only twenty minutes' flying time from the south coast of England, the political and military establishment in the United Kingdom recognized that the air posed a particular challenge to national defence and domestic security. One of the most immediate interests of the Committee for the Scientific Survey of Air Defence (CSSAD), convened to address the UK's particular aerial challenge and chaired by Sir Henry Tizard, was Germany's rumoured development of a so-called 'death ray'.

The existence of death rays, or death beams – weapons said to be capable of destroying entire towns via a beam of high-energy radio waves – had long been rumoured and speculated about. At various times, Guglielmo Marconi, Nikola Tesla and other, lesser-known radio innovators claimed to have developed just such a device, although none had been able to demonstrate working examples to the satisfaction of scientific or military communities in the United States or Great Britain. Quite the contrary, in fact. Claims about the production of death rays had, by the 1930s, become the stuff of confidence tricksters and charlatans who regularly attempted to fleece money out of British government ministries with the promise of new high-tech weapons. And yet the prospect of a weapon capable of destroying enemy aircraft long before they could impart damage or destruction continued to excite interest. Robert Watson-Watt (1892–1973), the head of the UK's National Physical Laboratory (NPL), was tasked with testing the

RADIO'S LIVEST MAGAZINE

RADIO WAVES KILL PLANT INSECTS

Radio's war with nature is the cover story on this issue of *Radio Craft*, 1934.

feasibility of such a device and was very quickly able to demonstrate its technological impossibility thanks to the swift calculations of a colleague, Arnold Wilkins (1907–1985). More productively, it was in the course of the conversations between Watt and Wilkins that the two men began considering the interaction of radio and airborne objects, and in particular, reports that aircraft had been observed to disrupt the reception of shortwave radio signals. When Watson-Watt reported back to the Tizard Committee in April 1935, it was on the subject of 'Detection and Location of Aircraft by Radio Methods'. While this might have been somewhat less exciting than the prospect of 'death rays', the scheme was well received by the committee and the Air Ministry was impressed by radio's strategic potential for accurately determining the position of aircraft in the skies before they were visible to even the most eagle-eyed observers, or their sound detected by the most sensitive acoustic locators.[15] After observing a series of top-secret tests at the

Robert Watson-Watt (1892–1973) with his experimental radar apparatus, 1957.

BBC's shortwave transmitter station in Daventry, the physicist A. P. Rowe coined the name Radio Direction and Finding (RDF) to describe this new application of radio. Today this system is better known by an acronym popularized by the U.S. navy and corporations during the Second World War. Watson-Watt had invented 'Radio Detection and Ranging', or RADAR (now simply 'radar').

Radar-guided searchlights are demonstrated in London's Hyde Park, 1945.

By June 1935, the UK's fledgling radar could detect aircraft 26 km (16 mi.) away; by the end of that year aircraft were 'visible' 96 km (60 mi.) from the English coast, rising to 161 km (100 mi.) by early 1936. In 1937, further innovations by Wilkins added the ability to measure the height above ground of approaching aircraft and by early 1938 the first five radar stations of what would become known as the UK's 'Chain Home' system were inaugurated for the protection of London.

Inside a Chain Home radar station during the Second World War.

The new strategic asset was put to use immediately by monitoring aerial activity during the Munich crisis of September 1938. When war in Europe did finally break out almost exactly a year later, Chain Home had 21 operational stations and the great majority of the UK's Atlantic and Channel coasts were under its umbrella. As the Battle for France came to a close with the evacuation from Dunkirk, and with a Battle of Britain looming, the Chain Home was stretched still further to cover the west coast of Great Britain and Ireland. Such was the quantity of information being gathered from these stations that whole new systems and structures of communications, with strict hierarchies, clear protocols and new modes of data visualization were needed to ensure that front-line gunnery operators and pilots received clear and timely locational data. The architectural and logistical outcomes of the Dowding system (named after Air Chief Marshal Hugh Dowding), in combination with Watson-Watt's radar, are now immortalized in great British war movies including *Angels One Five* (1952, dir. George More O'Ferrall) and *Battle of Britain* (1969, dir. Guy Hamilton).

Today radar plays a critical role in detecting and, in some cases, governing the movement of objects that collectively construct the modern world. Radar ensures passenger safety and the smooth operation of airports and aircraft around the world by underpinning air-traffic control systems, aircraft anti-collision systems and ground-controlled approach systems that aid pilots to land aircraft in low visibility and adverse weather conditions. Marine radar facilitates a similar smooth movement of ships and other maritime vessels by detecting the bearing and distance of ships, aiding navigation and assisting ships to fix their position at sea. In busy ports and harbour environments, 'vessel traffic service radar systems' monitor and regulate ship movements. Radar visualizations of our skies are shown daily as part of television weather forecasts, while providing meteorologists with essential data about impending thunderstorms, tornadoes, winter storms and heavy bands of precipitation. Radar, perhaps unsurprisingly given its wartime origins, has been embraced by military forces and

A U.S. sailor operates
the SPN-43 air search
radar on board USS
Wasp, 2012.

arms manufacturers and is integral to air-defence systems, antimissile
systems, drone programmes and devices such as proximity fuses.
Geologists and archaeologists have adapted radar for use within the
earth and use ground-penetrating radar to search for hidden objects
and to map the composition of the Earth's crust. Even this relatively
benign use of radar has been securitized along some of the world's
most challenging political frontiers, including the Korean 'DMZ'
(Demilitarized Zone) and the U.S.–Mexico and Israel–Gaza borders,
where the ground is systematically monitored to check for the presence of tunnels and the literal 'undermining' of border security. Radar
is a key component of autonomous driving systems and, as a result,
looks set to play a part in revolutionizing our cars, roads and cities,
and the way we travel, into the future.

　　Perhaps one of the most vexing uses of radar thus far was developed
by John L. Barker Sr and Ben Midlock during the Second World War.
In 1948 the two men turned their radar apparatus, originally designed

to aid the safe landing of aircraft, towards motor vehicles travelling on the roads of Connecticut in the United States. By measuring the changing frequencies of radio waves reflected from vehicles as they moved towards their radar – a phenomenon known as the Doppler effect – Barker and Midlock were able to determine with great accuracy the speed of the moving vehicles. The two men had invented the speed gun, and the eager Connecticut state police issued their first speeding fines based on radar technology in 1949. Speed guns, speed traps and speed cameras are now a ubiquitous part of motorists' lives around the world. Ironically, one notable casualty of the speed gun on the roads of Canada in the 1960s was none other than radar's inventor, Sir Robert Watson-Watt. When asked to pull over to receive his fine (£4 9s, approx. $12.50) from the police, Watt is reported to have said: 'My God, if I'd known what they were going to do with it,

An inspector for the Comprehensive Test Ban Treaty Organization uses ground-penetrating radar to detect sub-subsurface structural changes in Kazakhstan in 2008.

Buffalo police department's RADAR unit, 1974.

I'd never have invented it!' As he later recorded in a poem, this seemed 'A Rough Justice' for the father of radar:

> Pity Sir Watson-Watt,
> strange target of this radar plot
> and thus, with others I can mention,
> the victim of his own invention.
> His magical all-seeing eye
> enabled cloud-bound planes to fly
> but now by some ironic twist
> it spots the speeding motorist
> and bites, no doubt with legal wit,
> the hand that once created it.[16]

SPYING AND ESPIONAGE

Two men sit and observe a painting on the wall of London's National Gallery. Conversation is brief and awkward; the older man, clearly perturbed, starts to move off. The younger man says, slightly enquiringly, '007?', forestalling the older man's departure. 'I am your new Quartermaster.' As the scene unfolds, and in a time-honoured tradition familiar to book readers and film viewers the world over, 'Q' issues 007 with the essential tools required by cinema's most famous spy. Since the first James Bond film in 1962, audiences have become accustomed to Bond receiving ever-more elaborate gadgets from Q-branch: tear-gas-emitting attaché cases, watches with laser-cutting tools and other untold uses, exploding toothpaste and cars with an always-expanding range of capabilities. But in the spirit of the 'rebooted' and more back-to-basics Bond ushered in with the actor Daniel Craig, Q's offering on this occasion seems somewhat meagre. An aeroplane ticket to Shanghai, a Walther PPK (albeit with some modifications) and, lastly, 'a standard issue radio transmitter'. 'A gun and a radio,' Craig's Bond grudgingly notes, 'not exactly Christmas, is it?' For Bond aficionados, the combination of the Walther PPK and a radio provides a narrative reference back to some of the earliest Bond films, including *Dr No* (1962, dir. Terence Young), *From Russia with Love* (1963, dir. Terence Young) and *Goldfinger* (1964, dir. Guy Hamilton), invoking an era of relative technological innocence. In so doing, the makers of *Skyfall*

James Bond, played by Daniel Craig, receives his new miniature radio from Q in *Skyfall*, 2012.

(2012, dir. Sam Mendes) perhaps also revealed something of the remarkable timelessness in the technological imagination of spying and espionage. A gun first designed in 1929 and a radio transmitter with its technological origins at the turn of the twentieth century – and, of course, the body of Bond himself. 'Were you expecting an exploding pen?' Q replies. 'We don't really go in for that anymore.'

That radio's capacities for deception, misinformation and subterfuge were recognized from its earliest days is, perhaps, unsurprising. After all, radio exuded the qualities required for espionage. It was, first and foremost, invisible. For many, listening to radio allowed international borders to be crossed and enabled access to information from far-off places that was otherwise restricted, or may have been in conflict with the views or values of their own country. 'Listening in' to wireless signals was deeply personal and had an air of surveillance to it. Radio was furtive, secretive and was also highly technical. It was not for everyone – at least not at first. It relied on technical expertise, access to equipment and knowledge of a coded language – typically Morse – that would enable sender and receiver to communicate using dots and dashes. By the time of the First World War, radio's involvement in espionage had become well recognized and a further layer of coded encrypted messages transmitted through the air. This only further deepened the sense of mystery that surrounded radio.

Newspapers and more specialist 'wireless' publications, including Marconi's *Wireless World* and the U.S.-based *Electrical Experimenter*, were filled with articles that both celebrated radio's military application and warned of its potential for espionage. By spring 1918, U.S. newspapers were in the grips of all-out 'radio hysteria': their pages filled with stories of suspected German radio infiltration of the United States and the discovery of 'secret radio' and 'spy wireless' everywhere from the peaks of the Catskill Mountains to the tops of New York skyscrapers.

In one slightly earlier story from New York, in June 1917, the police department reported the arrest of a German spy who had seemingly been brought to their attention by a number of vigilant citizens. The

U. S. Government and Police Experts Were Much Surprised to Find That the Cabinet Here Shown, Which Was Recently Seized with Max Wax, a German Spy, Was Capable of Receiving Secret Radio Messages from Germany.

The 'remarkable' suitcase radio found in the possession of alleged German spy Max Wax, 1917.

man, who identified himself by the unlikely name of Max Hans Ludwig Wax, was found in possession of what was described as a 'little black box of mystery'. While Wax attempted to dismiss the object as a theatrical prop in a low-level con-trick, the New York police identified the object to be a fully operational radio set capable of receiving signals from as far away as Berlin, although only after the police officer in charge of the department's wireless station was called in to investigate. The device, we are told, defied easy identification. The 'contrivance' was configured in a 'queer arrangement' and didn't conform to any known radio receiver:

The box is about two and a half feet square. It is covered with black enamel and has silver handles and brass hinges and clasp. It must have cost at least $800, according to the estimate of experts.

The mystery of Wax's suitcase radio was only deepened when the police asked him to demonstrate its operation. 'He fingered several parts of the mechanism for a moment or two', it is reported, 'and finally succeeded in causing a short circuit, which effectually put the whole thing out of commission.'[17] Perhaps of greater concern to the U.S. authorities was that while the radio was indeed perfectly capable of receiving signals from continental Europe, it was only capable of transmitting over a 161-km (100-mi.) range – suggesting that Wax was

Packhorse used by U.S. Army Signal Corps, carrying a chest of instruments for wireless telegraphy, 1916.

PART OF FIELD OUTFIT FOR WIRELESS TELEGRAPH – U.S. ARMY SIGNAL CORPS 694-6
(CHEST CONTAINING INSTRUMENTS)

June   25 cents

Science and Invention

FORMERLY
ELECTRICAL EXPERIMENTER

How to build
A RADIO OUTFIT
IN YOUR SUITCASE
See Page 152

How to make a
homemade suitcase
radio in *Science and
Invention*, June 1922.
communicating with German U-boats off the U.S. eastern seaboard or
was perhaps part of a wider network of German spies. Later editions
of the *Electrical Experimenter* would recount tales of 'A War-time
Radio Detective' responsible for investigating possible signs of radio
espionage within the continental U.S. during the war, many of which
were false alarms but some of which were genuine cases of radio
intrigue. During the peak of radio hysteria, it was not unusual for
windmills and other perfectly innocent bits of agricultural and domestic apparatus to be misconstrued as potential threats to national
security by a hyper-vigilant public, especially so if they were owned or
administered by people of German descent.

One unfortunate casualty of this mounting radio hysteria was a
great icon of early radio experimentation. After several 'strangers' were
sighted around the mothballed site of Nikola Tesla's radio tower on
Long Island it was feared that spies might be harnessing the 56-m-tall
(185-ft) tower to transmit intelligence back to Germany. Rather than
tightening security around the site (which was already recognized as
an important landmark to a great pioneer of electromagnetism), the
federal government ordered the tower to be dynamited in 1917. The last
remnant of Tesla's experiments in 'wireless power' was eliminated in
the U.S. government's pursuit of domestic radio control and wartime
security.

If radio's dramatic potential was already apparent during the First
World War, this was only further magnified as radio's global reach was
more fully realized during subsequent global conflicts, and as radio
technologies became ever smaller, more portable and more discreet.
Widely used by the CIA and its Second World War predecessor, the
Office of Strategic Services (OSS), was the United States' own attempt
at the suitcase radio – the SSTR-1. In reality the SSTR-1 wasn't designed
to be solely contained within a suitcase at all. Reports suggest that the
dimensions of the power supply were carefully selected so they could
be discreetly inserted inside 'a European loaf of bread' (as demonstrated
by an in-house OSS instructional film from around 1943) while on

mobile operations, although the carrier evidently needed to wear a large overcoat to disguise the bulk of the radio apparatus itself. The James Bond novels and films would, of course, provide the archetype for the blurring of spy-fiction and spy-fact and was successful largely thanks to Ian Fleming's own experiences working for the British secret intelligence services during the Second World War. The tracking device designed to fit inside the heel of Bond's shoe in *Goldfinger*, for example, is strikingly prescient of the discovery in the early 1970s of highly specialized radio-operated listening devices that had been inserted inside the shoe heels of at least one U.S. diplomat stationed in Eastern Europe. These battery-powered 'drop transmitters' seem to have been inserted into diplomatic footwear during routine repairs. As one U.S. newspaper reported in 1972, 'the diplomat wore his shoes to work, unaware he was a walking broadcasting station.' He was, we are a told, 'a Diplomat on the air'.[18] A very similar pair of shoes can be seen in the International Spy Museum in Washington, DC. During the 1970s and 1980s, the Bond franchise continued its fascination with radio, particularly where those radios could be disguised within other banal items. In 1973's *Live and Let Die* (dir. Guy Hamilton) we see radio transmitters inserted inside a villain's flute, a clothing brush and the

A drop transmitter planted by the Romanian Secret Services into a U.S. diplomat's shoe.

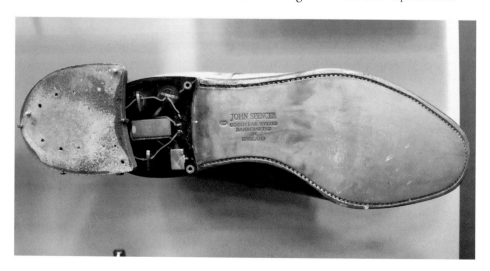

A James Bond gadget
for the 1980s: the
'ghetto blaster' is
tested by the MI6
boffins in *The Living
Daylights* (1987).

A James Bond gadget
for the 1980s: the
'ghetto blaster' is
tested by the MI6
boffins in *The Living
Daylights* (1987).

cigarette lighter of a CIA vehicle; a CIA agent's purse in *Moonraker* (1979, dir. Lewis Gilbert); Bond's Q-branch supplied wristwatches in both *For Your Eyes Only* (1981, dir. John Glen) and *Octopussy* (1983, dir. John Glen) – the latter of which is also capable of tracking the direction of a homing device placed inside a Fabergé egg; and the handle of a very workaday gardener's rake in *Licence to Kill* (1989, dir. John Glen). In *The Living Daylights* (1987, dir. John Glen), the fifteenth Bond instalment and the first to feature Timothy Dalton as the eponymous spy, it is an apparently benign radio set that is used as the disguise for Q's latest covert technology. Reflecting the spirit of the age, we see the ultimate symbol of 1980s urban music culture – the boom box – transform with the press of a button into a shoulder-mounted rocket launcher. 'Something we're making for the Americans', Q announces. 'We call it a ghetto blaster'.

In May 1960, an American U2 spy plane, being flown at more than 18,288 m (60,000 ft), was shot down over Russia. The pilot, Gary Powers, survived the crash, was interrogated by the KGB, tried for espionage and imprisoned for nearly two years until his release under a prisoner exchange deal with the U.S. in 1962. While Russian mastery of radio was crucial to the targeting of Powers's aeroplane and the guidance controls of the S-75 Dvina missile system that had brought him down, the 'U2 incident' became a focal point for an intense diplomatic dispute between the United States and Soviet Union over instances of spying, espionage and sabotage. Soviet foreign minister Andrei Gromyko used the physical incursion of the U2 into Russian airspace to accuse the United States of 'perfidy' and 'subterfuge'. The U.S. counter-charged with their own detailed account of eleven Soviet spies discovered operating within the U.S. over the previous seven years. In some senses, neither of these charges were particularly revelatory. Espionage and counter-espionage had, after all, become key weapons of military conflict since the First World War and were actively pursued strategies in the Cold War confrontation.

The U2 incident did provoke one major revelation, however. Speaking at the UN on 26 May 1962, the U.S. ambassador, Henry Cabot Lodge, Jr, defended the use of the U2 by vividly demonstrating Russia's complicity in Cold War clandestine surveillance and in the development of advanced electronic eavesdropping technologies. To help make his point to the gathered UN delegates, Lodge called for an object to be displayed by a State Department official. The circular object, perhaps 61 cm (2 ft) in diameter, was a deeply carved and highly decorative wooden copy of the Great Seal of the United States – the kind of object that would not look out of place in state houses or courtrooms across the United States. This particular carving, however, had been gifted to the then U.S. ambassador to Russia, Averell Harriman (1891–1986), by a Russian youth organization in August 1945 as a gesture of post-war friendship, and had hung in the library of the ambassador's official Moscow residence, Spaso House. To the audible amusement of the UN delegates, Lodge lifted the front panel from the seal to reveal an internal cavity and a hidden device. Little did the Americans know at the time of its presentation in 1945, the carving contained a revolutionary kind of radio bugging device that required no external power supply or any kind of wired connection through the supporting wall. Instead, the device was activated – *illuminated* – by a strong radio signal from an external source, which powered and operated it. These characteristics meant that the bug had a potentially unlimited life and was almost impossible to detect using conventional counter-measures. The seal, and the bugging device, hung on the wall of Spaso House undetected for seven years. It survived three different u.s. ambassadors and was only discovered in 1952. The u.s. media added to the sense of Cold War intrigue and mystery by dubbing the device 'The Thing', invoking the Alien-like presence of Howard Hawkes's 1952 science-fiction thriller of the same name. In reality the device has very human origins. It was later revealed that the Great Seal bug had been designed by the Soviet inventor Leon Theremin (1896–1993), who is today perhaps better remembered as the inventor of an electronic music device that bears his name and which was popularized by the likes of Dmitri Shostakovich (1906–1975) and later used by the Beach Boys in their hit song 'Good Vibrations' (1966).

Almost thirty years after the collapse of the Soviet Union, radio's Cold War continues to reverberate within the international airwaves.

Revealing the inner workings of the Great Seal bug at the UN, 1960.

The campaign to free the Cuban Five, arrested in 1998 and convicted of international radio espionage in 2000.

Number stations – shortwave radio stations that transmit blocks of synthetically voiced numbers – are an eerie electromagnetic legacy of an era when spies and foreign agents were embedded deep behind enemy lines and were reliant on radio to receive their secret instructions. At the height of the Cold War many hundreds of number stations broadcast their particular coded messages on precisely timed schedules and became identifiable by distinct call signs. One of the best-known number stations was nicknamed the Lincolnshire Poacher – because each transmission was prefaced with the opening bars of the old English folk song of the same name. Reports suggest that the Lincolnshire Poacher began its transmissions at some point in the 1970s and closed in July 2008, during which time it broadcast initially from UK government-controlled transmitters in Buckinghamshire before ultimately moving to the Royal Air Force base at Akrotiri in Cyprus for the primary purpose of serving British agents in the Middle East. The Cuban number station Atención came to some international prominence during the trial of the so-called 'Cuban Five' on charges of espionage against the United States between 2000 and 2001. In presenting their evidence to the jury in Miami, the U.S. government detailed three Atención messages successfully decoded using computer programmes found in the group's possession. The five were convicted of conspiracy to commit espionage, conspiracy to commit murder, and of acting as agents of a foreign government. Between them, the Cuban Five served more than sixty years in the U.S. prison system. The final three detainees were repatriated to Cuba as part of a prisoner exchange in 2014.

6
RADIO AND POPULAR CULTURE

E stimates suggest that there may be upwards of 40,000 radio stations in active operation around the world – although this is necessarily a rough estimate due to the operation of countless 'illegal' and informal stations. The worldwide commercial radio industry, which is dominated by fewer and larger media conglomerates (and their national subdivisions) integrated by the commercial trade in radio programme formats, was worth U.S.$43.7 billion in 2015, with Asia-Pacific and Latin America recognized as significant growth markets for the future.[1] Shrugging off the threat of television and the Internet, radio can now be consumed via a raft of new listening platforms and delivery technologies, such as digital audio broadcasting (DAB), digital satellite radio services and via Internet streaming. It is also not unusual now to 'watch', somewhat counterintuitively, radio programmes live on digital televisions, often animated with webcams of the broadcasting studios. The radio industry's embrace of broadcast and production technologies has led to the emergence of more specialist, interest-driven networks, while 'mainstream' programming around the radio world has arguably become more homogeneous because of the global trade in programme 'formats' and the globalization of popular music.

Radio has been instrumental in the emergence of popular culture and has, in turn, been picked up, reflected, critiqued, satirized and valorized in literature, films, television – and through radio itself. Before radio, live 'audiences' needed to be in the physical proximity of the object requiring their attention – whether a lecturer, a troupe of actors or a group of musicians – and this ultimately limited the size of an audience based on the audibility of the sound that could be produced in a particular theatre, musical hall or stadium. While the advent of radio didn't ensure the construction of truly 'popular cultures', it brought with it the possibility of, and the commercial requirement for, mass audiences exposed to the same experience and at the same time – and the emergence of shared tastes in literature, poetry or anything else that might be broadcast over the air.

THE MADE AND UNMADE CONNECTION

Over the past century, radio has not only reshaped our lives, reconfigured our homes and brought about an era of mass media and mass entertainment, it has entered the popular imagination and provided us with new ways – and new words – to help us engage with the wider world. Such words include 'broadcasting', which up until the early 1920s was used purely in reference to a farming technique for scattering seeds across a field, but was adopted to describe the technique for spreading radio waves across even more vast geographical spaces, and has been stretched to help us understand a truly global electromagnetic phenomenon. Broadcasting has, of course, adapted to and survived the rise of television, unlike the term 'Hertzian waves' and even, to some extent, 'radio waves', which have been slowly superseded in popular usage by the rather vaguer 'airwaves' since the 1970s. As already discussed, the very British use of the term 'wireless' had already succumbed to the punchier Americanism of 'radio' throughout most parts of British society when Professor Alan S. C. Ross and Nancy Mitford were popularizing their linguistic class-indicators in the mid-1950s – although, as Ross noted in his original 1953 paper, demonstrating anything other than contempt for wireless/radio was quite enough to mark one out as 'non-U':

There are, it is true, still a few minor points of life which may serve to demarcate the upper class, but they are only minor ones. The games of real tennis and pique, an aversion to high tea, having one's cards engraved (not printed), not playing tennis in braces, and, in some cases, a dislike of certain comparatively modern inventions such as the telephone, the cinema and the wireless are still perhaps marks of the upper class.[2]

The Sower, a marble sculpture by Eric Gill (1882–1940), resides in the Art Deco lobby of BBC Broadcasting House.

In order for a particular radio station to become audible through our radio sets we are required to 'tune' our receivers to a precise wavelength or frequency, a process that commonly involves the physical act of turning a dial or operating a digital interface. This association between audibility, intelligibility and 'tuning in' now forms the basis of a range of radio-related metaphorical devices that have permeated the English language over the past century. We might say, for example, that we were attempting to 'tune in to a conversation' if we are struggling to hear our friends or colleagues in particularly noisy surroundings. Conversely, if we become distracted during a meeting we might apologize for momentarily 'tuning out'. If we are fortunate enough to meet someone with whom we have lots in common, you might say that you are 'on the same frequency' or 'on the same wavelength' as the other person. More often, however, these kinds of idioms are invoked when we struggle to 'tune in' or find ourselves on a somewhat 'different wavelength' to those around us, and in that sense radio provides us with a range of communications-related metaphors that help to make sense of interpersonal contact and the made and *unmade* 'connection'. If you lose contact with another person, or if, for example, a company fails to respond to emails or telephone calls, we might complain of their 'radio silence' or share our frustration by complaining that they have 'gone off the radar'. Radar has proven, in itself, to be a remarkably flexible metaphorical device. If we seek to do something with a certain degree of subtlety or wish our personal involvement to go largely unnoticed, we might say that we are attempting to 'fly under the radar', but, equally,

if we wish to demonstrate our complete awareness of a situation, or an upcoming event, we might say that 'it's very much on my radar'.

Just as radio has entered our everyday language, so the film and television industries have embraced radios as similarly everyday, background objects that lend a sense of realism to the lived environments and human lives we see depicted on screen – providing, in many cases, a spoken or musical soundtrack to daily tasks around the home, or as accompaniment to road movies. Occasionally, though, both radio's physical and its more immaterial qualities have been deployed as powerful audio-visual metaphors as well as lending considerable dramatic potential.

Reflecting Cold War nuclear anxieties, films like *Fail-Safe* (1964, dir. Sidney Lumet) and *Crimson Tide* (1995, dir. Tony Scott) confront viewers with the potentially shocking consequences of human

The hand-cranked BC-778 emergency radio transmitter, as used in *Island in the Sky* (1953), was known as 'Gibson Girl' by U.S. aircrews because of its narrow waistline.

over-reliance on technology in the nuclear age, especially so when that technology fails. In *Fail-Safe*, the U.S. long-range bomber fleet are revealed to be equipped with a radio-based 'fail-safe' mechanism that should, in theory, prevent them from launching their nuclear payloads without a coded confirmation directly from the U.S. president. However, as the film proceeds, we come to learn that 'go code' has been mistakenly transmitted to one bomber group, which the U.S. military are then unable to rescind due to interference from powerful Soviet radio-jamming technologies. Radio's failures, and the Cold War battle for electromagnetic superiority, put the world on the brink of nuclear catastrophe. *Crimson Tide* pursues similar concerns, albeit in the context of a U.S. nuclear submarine, the USS *Alabama*, that is brought to the state of peak nuclear readiness only to lose radio contact with its strategic command, sparking a tense interpersonal stand-off between the *Alabama*'s trigger-happy captain and the boat's more cerebral executive officer. Nuclear disaster is only averted thanks to a last-gasp effort by the submarine's radio engineer to re-establish radio communications, which he does with only moments to spare.

Radio's presence, and then sudden absence, withdrawal or failure, has become a commonly used trope to heighten senses of isolation from the wider world, especially in the Robinsonade genre of island castaways and other survival adventures, such as the films *Island in the Sky* (1953, dir. William A. Wellman), *Six Days, Seven Nights* (1998, dir. Ivan Reitman) and the true-life drama *Alive* (1993, dir. Frank Marshall). Inspired by the 1972 Andes flight disaster, *Alive* reveals the unsuccessful attempt by the survivors to re-establish contact with the outside world by rewiring the aeroplane's radio beacon, and ultimately the torment of hearing on their surviving radio receiver that a search and rescue mission to find them had been called off – events that, together, prompt the survivors to cannibalize the corpses of the dead. The British war film *Where Eagles Dare* (1968, dir. Brian G. Hutton), based on the novel by Alistair MacLean, tells the story of a crack team of Allied operatives dropped into the snow-covered

Austrian Alps for the apparent purpose of infiltrating the regional headquarters of the German high command. Radio is a recurring motif throughout the film, and an important narrative device. Making regular contact with their commanders back in Britain is a crucial part of the group's mission, and the team's backpack-sized radio set and much-repeated radio call signs are important visual and aural markers of the film. 'Broadsword calling Danny Boy', as spoken by the actor Richard Burton (1925–1984), is now one of the most oft-quoted lines from twentieth-century cinema. Switching to a more comedic register, U.S. television viewers from 1964 could hardly miss the weekly travails of the hapless (and now culturally iconic) Gilligan on the CBS show, *Gilligan's Island*. Over 98 episodes, the show followed the comic misadventures of seven ill-matched island castaways and their attempts to escape their island prison. Much of the humour, and even more of the plot development, came in the form of the ensemble's responses

Richard Burton, as Major John Smith, tries to send out an emergency message in *Where Eagles Dare* (1968).

to daily Hawaiian news broadcasts they received on their iconic Packard Bell AR-851 radio receiver.

Members of the cast of TV's *Gilligan's Island* (1964–92), together with their trusty Packard Bell radio (foreground) and a homemade CB radio in 1966.

The often-powerful connections between broadcasters and their audiences has been widely explored in television and movies. In 1987's *Good Morning, Vietnam*, discussed in an earlier chapter, it was the transformative effect of a fictionalized version of the DJ, Adrian Cronauer (famously portrayed by Robin Williams), on beleaguered U.S. military personnel during the Vietnam War. In the films *Play*

Misty for Me (1971, dir. Clint Eastwood) and *Talk Radio* (1988, dir. Oliver Stone), the connections between broadcaster and listener take on much more troubling and sinister qualities when listeners pursue violent campaigns against 'on-air' personalities. *Talk Radio* was informed by the real-life assassination of the Denver-based talk radio DJ Alan Berg by a white supremacist group, the White Order, in 1984.

GHOSTS, VOICES AND THE RADIO UNCANNY

For many of the earliest radio pioneers, the theoretical existence of radio waves provoked profound questions about the nature of the air, the atmosphere and the possibility that there existed an invisible medium through which radio waves travelled – a substance that connected all human beings together. Borrowing from ancient Greek and Roman natural philosophies that had sought to explain phenomena such as the motion of light and gravity and the existence of the so-called 'fifth element', there emerged a suite of late nineteenth-century theories that postulated the existence of this space-filling substance using the same classical name: the ether. This was certainly not a marginal interest within the scientific establishment or the sole preserve of crank scientists. In reality, ether theory was accepted by practically all physicists up to the end of the nineteenth century. It was mainstream science and was entirely sensible in the context of contemporary physics. Isaac Newton (1642–1727) assumed the existence of an ether in *The Third Book of Opticks*, published in 1704:

> Doth not this aethereal medium in passing out of water, glass, crystal, and other compact and dense bodies in empty spaces, grow denser and denser by degrees, and by that means refract the rays of light not in a point, but by bending them gradually in curve lines?

William Thomson (today better remembered as Lord Kelvin and for his role in masterminding the laying of the first transatlantic telegraph

Eric Bogosian as
Barry Champlain in
Talk Radio (1988).

cable) was a firm believer in the ether throughout his scientific career. James Clerk Maxwell, who had (as we have already seen) demonstrated the 'unification' of light and electromagnetic radiation as expressions of the same physical phenomenon (in 1864) and is considered one of the finest theoretical physicists of all time, was similarly enamoured with the concept of an all-connecting ether – as was clear in his 1873 *Treatise on Electricity and Magnetism*, in which he notes:

> In several parts of this treatise an attempt has been made to explain electromagnetic phenomena by means of mechanical action transmitted from one body to another by means of a medium occupying the space between them. The undulatory theory of light also assumes the existence of a medium. We have now to show that the properties of the electromagnetic medium are identical with those of the luminiferous [that is, light-bearing] medium.

Radio waves, according to Maxwell, not only relied on the ether as their carrying medium, but also provided a potential means of proving its existence as a truly universal connecting substance. Of course, no such proof was ever found. The scientific downfall of ether began with the Michelson–Morley experiment (1887), which completely failed to detect the presence of the predicted 'aether wind', and Einstein's 1905 prediction that light exists as both a wave and a particle (what we now call photons). And yet, the association of a universally connecting ether and the phenomenon of electromagnetism (and radio waves, in particular) sparked considerable interest and excitement in *fin-de-siècle* society and popular culture, and this is a productive association that continues to resonate in popular culture even today. The ether, with radio as its mediator, was filled with dramatic as well as scientific potential.

In the comparatively little-known short story 'Wireless' (1902), Rudyard Kipling – better known for the likes of *The Jungle Book* (1894) and *Kim* (1901) – explored the rather more ethereal themes of transcendental and dream-like communication between the living and the dead. 'Wireless' is set within a pharmacist's shop somewhere along England's south coast during an evening of wireless radio experimentation. Three men get together in order to use radio apparatus to listen in to wireless transmissions coming from a nearby experimental wireless station in the town of Poole. One of the men, we are led to understand, is terminally ill (probably with tuberculosis) and during the night becomes increasingly feverish and somewhat intoxicated with homemade medication. In one key scene, Mr Cashell, the wireless enthusiast of the group, establishes an unexpected wireless contact – with apparently related effects on both the story's narrator and the terminally ill Mr John Shaynor:

> 'Hsh!' said Mr. Cashell guardedly from the inner office, as though in the presence of spirits. 'There's something coming through from somewhere; but it isn't Poole.' I heard the crackle of sparks as he depressed the keys of the transmitter. In my own brain, too, something crackled, or it might have been the hair on my head. Then

I heard my own voice, in a harsh whisper: 'Mr. Cashell, there is something coming through here, too. Leave me alone till I tell you.'³

In the lines that follow, it becomes clear that in the same moment of heightened electromagnetic activity (as evidenced by the sparks of the wireless receiver) the dying Mr Shaynor has somehow been transformed into a human receiver of ethereal and other-worldly communication. As with the radio apparatus, Shaynor's signals don't have their origins in Poole but instead seem to represent a spiritual channelling of the English Romantic poet John Keats (1795–1821). In his delirium, Shaynor stutteringly pens the words to Keats's 'The Eve of St Agnes' (1820), despite claiming on his return to full consciousness to have never read Keats. While Kipling's true intent in 'Wireless' has been subject to considerable debate and critique (as, too, have been the trustworthiness of both Shaynor and the narrator), what is more certain is that Kipling is reflecting here some very particular late Victorian fantasies and fascinations: radio's seemingly uncanny abilities in plucking voices out of the air; a belief in the idea of the all-connecting ether; and a particular Victorian enthusiasm for the paranormal and other-worldly. Although not a spiritualist himself (in fact Kipling became a noted critic of spiritualism), many late Victorian scholars, scientists and public figures were persuaded of the continuation and evolution of the human spirit even after physical, bodily, death. One popular theory espoused by some spiritualists, including the noted physicist Oliver Lodge, suggested the ether as the medium within which deceased human spirits were sustained, and in that sense radio waves and human spirits were believed to both occupy the same all-connecting substance and share similar qualities and characteristics. Both represented particular forms of invisible energies that could be detected with the right kinds of apparatus and expertise. While Lodge didn't necessarily believe 'wireless' radio waves to be the mechanism of choice for such spiritual communication, there was certainly a collision in the underlying 'science' (of the ether, for example) and supporting

Celebrity spiritualists
and 'ether theory'
exponents, Lady
Jean and Sir Arthur
Conan Doyle,
c. 1920.

metaphors (such as 'mediums') that blurred this boundary in the popular imagination. Kipling's 'Wireless' represents one manifestation of that blurring to the extent that some have even speculated that the narrator character might in fact be a thinly disguised caricature of another noted spiritualist, and close friend of Lodge, Sir Arthur Conan Doyle.

Even as belief in the ether was waning (a shift that would ultimately leave the likes of Lodge intellectually stranded), radio's uncanny qualities and behaviours continued to inspire fascination in the nascent technology. Radio's relationship and interaction with the human body continued to be the subject of notable intrigue long after Kipling's account of Mr Shaynor's electromagnetic possession in 'Wireless'. Some believed that the human body could function as both transmitter and receiver of electromagnetic radiation, and the readers of the *Literary Digest* were encouraged in 1928 to 'interact' with their wireless sets by forming human chains to enhance the effectiveness of their antennae – although the visual depiction provided in the magazine looks eerily like the kind of spiritualist soirée frequented by Lodge or Conan Doyle. Newspapers reported on the invention of new radio devices that promised to link 'the living and dead', and the live transmission of 'radio séances'.[4] The most widely publicized of these radio séances came in 1936 when Beatrice Houdini, the widow of the eponymous magician and illusionist Harry Houdini, announced a plan to 'raise the ghost of her dead husband by national radio broadcast' on the tenth anniversary of his death. The event, it was reported, would involve a 'coast-to-coast radio hookup, with séances in all parts of the country'. While this might seem to have been a somewhat straightforward tale of a grieving wife's desperate attempt to contact her deceased husband, the scheme was – perhaps appropriately – something of an illusion. During his lifetime, Harry Houdini had been an outspoken critic of spiritualism and had exposed the fraudulent practices of a number of high-profile mediums, including Jean Conan Doyle, the wife of Arthur Conan Doyle, who claimed to have successfully channelled the spirit of Houdini's dead mother. Even though this exposé brought about an end to Houdini's unlikely friendship with the creator of Sherlock Holmes, this was a mission he continued to pursue until, and even beyond, his untimely death in 1926. Before he died, Houdini agreed with Beatrice that if he found it possible to communicate with her in the afterlife he would use the code words 'Rosabelle believe' to establish his (and the medium's) authenticity, although more in the hope that the failure of mediums to identify the code would aid in their unmasking. After hosting annual séances over the nine years following her husband's death, Mrs Houdini sought to harness the additional power of radio to extend the 'psychic chain' and produce 'a final and conclusive test of the validity of claims of spiritualists'. On the night of the final Houdini séance, the long-deceased magician's spirit was 'invoked' for well over an hour. Despite the sobs and raised voices that begged Houdini to appear, no contact was made and no messages were received, leading Mrs Houdini to very publicly announce, once and for all, that 'spirit communication in any form is impossible.'[5]

Perhaps the most strange and uncanny radio stories related to the 'ghostly' action of wireless signals on the most mundane objects in the most banal and everyday circumstances. During the 1920s and 1930s, newspapers and magazines on both sides of the Atlantic regularly featured stories of strange radio-related occurrences and even the presence of 'radio ghosts'. In one such story from Bellmore, Long Island, in 1928, the owner of a particularly historic farmhouse reported 'radio ghosts' that caused 'voices and music to come apparently from the walls themselves'. In further investigations, the reporter determined that the reports weren't only 'true' but also 'understated'. As the reporter continued:

> at first faintly, swelling later in volume until every word was clear, a lecture voice was heard coming from the south wall of the room. The voice had an uncanny quality, unlike radio as

A human radio
antenna, as suggested
by *Literary Digest*
in 1928.

HUMAN CHAIN ACTING AS A RADIO ANTENNA .

received on either a tube or crystal set, but more like the tone of
the earliest phonograph.

This was followed a short time later by the sounds of a soprano singer
and a piano tinkling 'in the wall'.[6] Other reports told of an elevator in Des
Moines, Iowa, that would mysteriously play radio music, and a coal
shovel in Sweden that would occasionally break into song.[7] The widely
read U.S. magazine *Popular Science* reported in 1935 that 'weird electrical freaks' had been 'traced to runaway radio waves'. In a remarkably
alarming article that warned of the risks associated with 'superpower
broadcasting stations, saturating the atmosphere with energy', the
magazine confronted its readership with uncanny and downright
weird happenings in Mason, Ohio, after the opening of a 500,000-watt
radio transmitter:

> An ordinary-looking waterspout at the corner of a farmhouse hums
> the strains of a symphony, or declaims a dramatic bit from a play.
> A tin roof, next door, makes political speeches, or bursts into song.
> Inquire among the farmers of the neighbourhood, and nearly all
> will tell you of hearing these mysterious, ghostly voices issuing from
> inanimate things.[8]

Radio continues to intrigue for its uncanny ability to make unlikely connections across vast global, and even extra-terrestrial, spaces, while also being deployed as a narrative device in literature and cinema to explore other more spiritual and extra-dimensional connections. Radio's role in the 'long-range' detection of ghoulish events is one particular recurring trope. In the U.S.–Italian thriller *Qualcuno in ascolto/ High Frequency* (1988, dir. Faliero Rosati), two amateur radio hams, one in the U.S. and the other high in the Swiss Alps, happen to witness a murder via a rogue television signal during a thunderstorm and commit to solving the mystery and warning the next victim. The two characters slowly untangle the mystery, becoming radio detectives, and are ultimately able to meet in person. In the film *Frequency* (2000, dir. Gregory Hoblit), a Heathkit ham-radio set becomes the channel of communication between a son, John, and his long-deceased father, Frank, during a particularly powerful episode of the aurora borealis. Not only is John able to forewarn radio enthusiast Frank of the circumstances of his own death in a house fire (thereby allowing him to survive), but by combining forces and sharing information across a thirty-year timespan, the two characters are able to solve a series of murders (including that of John's mother) and ultimately protect their family in the past and present.

Radio bridges space and time in *Frequency* (2000).

In *Aningaaq* (2013) an Inuit fisherman has a conversation with a dying astronaut who is stranded in space.

The interdimensional communication explored in *Frequency* reson-ates strongly with Kipling's 'Wireless' and other stories such as John Wilson's 'Sparks' (1911), in which a maritime wireless operator, Harry, is separated from his lover by distance and then by her untimely death. The two estranged lovers are mysteriously reconnected many years later via an eerie radio signal that comes through Harry's wire-less set during a strange atmospheric event in the middle of the Pacific Ocean. Unlike in recent movies that are pleasantly resolved with the reunification of divided families, or the meeting of radio friends, 'Sparks' concludes somewhat more tragically when the story's narra-tor reports the death of the wireless operator to the ship's captain, revealing that the long-parted lovers have, ultimately, been reunited in 'the beyond'.

The Greenlandic short film *Aningaaq* (2013, dir. Jonás Cuarón), a companion piece to the multimillion-dollar blockbuster *Gravity* (2013, dir. Alfonso Cuarón), is similarly poignant in its examination of isolation, loneliness, death, the comfort of communication and the uncanny qualities of radio. The seven-minute film opens on the icy Sikvivitsoq fjord in Greenland, where an indigenous hunter is fishing and caring for his family. Suddenly his ham radio catches his attention as it sparks to life. A mayday distress call from a dying astronaut, depleted of oxygen, can be heard in English. Speaking only Greenlandic, Aningaaq cannot understand the full implications of the astronaut's situation and yet the two people – separated by language, culture, the Earth's atmosphere and perhaps thousands of kilometres – are connected as Aningaaq talks about his life and his fears (his dog is dying), and through his overheard interactions with his wife and young baby. He recites a Greenlandic lullaby and as the baby begins to sleep, so the astronaut also fades away. 'Are you there?', asks Aningaaq when he returns to his radio. There is no answer. Assuming that the connection with his momentary radio companion has been lost as easily as it was made, Aningaaq tosses down his radio microphone and returns to family life unaware of the comfort and solace that his radio voice has brought to the astronaut on the brink of death.

SPORTING LIFE

As I sit in my office on the outskirts of London in early summer and allow myself a brief moment to tune into the radio sitting on my desk, it is almost impossible to avoid the presence of sport. There are the dedicated sports radio stations from commercial providers and the BBC, such as talkSPORT and talkSPORT 2, BBC Radio 5 Live and its 'Sports Extra' spin-off, and others that are temporarily committed to the live coverage of particular sporting events (such as BBC Radio 4 on longwave). But sport has also come to colonize the airwaves by pervading radio programmes on music and general-interest topics as part of news and sports updates, conversations between DJs and presenters, call-in shows and on-air competitions. Even the weather forecast isn't immune from the long reach of sport. 'The roof will be closed at Wimbledon' is a modern portent of rain for radio audiences in London and the southeast of England. This weekend, as I write this, UK listeners are being promised a 'big weekend of sport', with live radio coverage of tennis from Wimbledon, test match cricket from Lord's, Formula One motor-racing, live updates from the Tour de France, and countless other local and regional sporting attractions. Sport on radio is hugely popular and big business, even in an era of multi-channel, high-definition television, and its appeal to large audiences was evident from the early 1920s.

American radio stations were the first to embrace sport as a worthy subject for broadcast. The first live sports commentary took place on 11 April 1921 with a lightweight boxing match between Johnny Dundee and Johnny Ray on KDKA in the Pittsburgh area of Pennsylvania. Florent Gibson of the *Pittsburgh Star* newspaper announced the ten-round bout, although no winner was declared as both men were still standing at the final bell. Baseball followed within a few months, when KDKA broadcast the Pittsburgh Pirates' victory over the Philadelphia Phillies from Forbes Field. Just a day later, live commentary on the Davis Cup match between Australia and Great Britain heralded two new firsts: radio's first tennis commentary, and the first broadcast of an *international* sporting competition. Harold Arlin, a former Westinghouse engineer, commentated on many of these pioneering broadcasts and in so doing became the world's first professional broadcast sports announcer. In the commercially driven world of U.S. radio, the success of these broadcasts pointed towards large audiences, increased radio sales, new revenue streams from advertising and, inevitably, more competition.

In the United Kingdom, it was anxieties about competition that seemed to be holding radio back from sports broadcasting. The press barons, in particular, were fearful that live commentaries and the transmissions of sports results would decimate sales of their newspapers. Elsewhere around the British 'Empire', progress was somewhat quicker. Cricket and rugby commentaries were first heard in the Sydney area of Australia in 1922 and 1924 respectively, and horse racing was broadcast from Melbourne in 1923. In Canada, the national sport of ice hockey

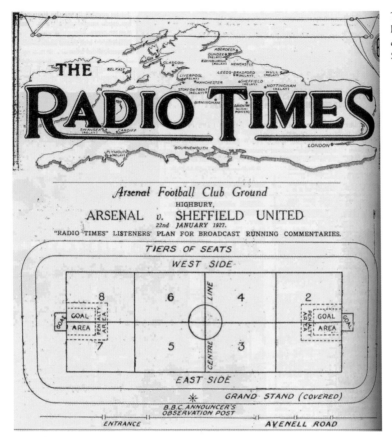

The BBC's short-lived football 'grid', designed by Lance Sieveking, 1927.

took to the air for the first time in February 1923 when a sports reporter for the *Toronto Star* provided a play-by-play commentary for the newspaper's own CFCA station. As the *Star* reported the following day: 'The announcer who described the play was right by the side of the rink and as he spoke, his voice was shot into space.'[9] Rugby commentaries followed in South Africa in 1924, and in New Zealand in 1926. The first live commentary on a field sport anywhere in Europe took place in August 1926 during the All-Ireland hurling semi-final between Kilkenny and Galway.

The awarding of a royal charter to the BBC (and its conversion into a public corporation) in January 1927 brought with it permission to undertake live sports commentaries, which it did almost immediately. A rugby international from Twickenham came first, followed slightly later in January by a live football (soccer) commentary of Arsenal versus Sheffield United from Highbury in north London. The BBC producer in charge, Lance Sieveking, was sufficiently concerned about the experience of listening to football that he devised an ingenious method to aid in the audience's spatial visualization of the game. In the days leading up to the game, the BBC listings magazine, *Radio Times*, published a plan of a football pitch divided into eight numbered squares. During the live commentary, a second voice was heard announcing the numbered square in which the action was taking place, and allowing the audience at home to plot the position of the ball. As popular as this was for early radio listeners, the BBC dropped the grid scheme in the mid-1930s as commentators became more confident and skilled in their 'calling'. Today Sieveking's comparatively short-lived innovation is widely credited (albeit incorrectly) as the source of the familiar phrase 'back to square one' – the result, perhaps, of rather over-active radio mythologizing.

Around the world television has come to dominate in the arena of sports broadcasting, particularly so following the growth of pay-to-view television channels and the meteoric rise in the cost of acquiring television rights from governing bodies and rights holders. The escalating cost of watching sport has led more recently to something of a radio renaissance as price-conscious sports fans in even the most developed nations turn back to free-to-air radio for their sporting entertainment. In the UK, this process has been aided by the gradual weakening of so-called sporting 'crown jewel' protections, and their loss from terrestrial to pay television channels. Cricket fans will know all too well the instrumental theme music that not only heralds each transmission of the BBC's *Test Match Special* programme but also the start of the summer season. *TMS* has been in continuous production since 1957 and can today be heard on 198 LW, on digital radio and via online streaming. The now often-replayed commentary from 1991 of the dismissal of English all-rounder Ian Botham (due to the unfortunate fact that he 'didn't quite get his leg over' his own wicket) has been voted the greatest piece of sports commentary of all time in audience polls in the United Kingdom. *TMS* also has the capacity to stir political passions, having been the subject of an Early Day Motion in the House of Commons in 2005 that called upon the BBC to preserve *Test Match Special*'s unique character and status as a 'much-loved institution'.[10]

RADIO GA GA

Over the past century, radio has become synonymous with one particular art form more than any other and that, of course, is music. Radio has shaped musical tastes around the world, made stars of musical performers, been at the leading edge of evolving musical genres, and developed programme formats exclusively for the delivery of music programming. Today, airtime on the radio can make or break the fortunes of musicians, eager to get their music heard.

In the UK, the genesis-point of music programming can be traced to one spectacular, experimental wireless broadcast that took place in 1920 involving the most famous operatic singer of the day, and perhaps one of the most iconic musical performers of all time. While Dame Nellie Melba is now immortalized through our consumption of the multiple culinary specialities named in her honour by Auguste Escoffier (including Peach Melba and Melba Toast), in broadcasting history she is remembered for lending her voice to the first musical broadcast ever to have taken place in the British Isles. Dame Nellie's recital, which was so pioneering that it preceded the creation of the British Broadcasting Company by two years, sparked with both modernity and traditionalism. The great soprano incorporated popular favourites, a suite of arias in English, French and Italian, and, of course, the British national anthem (to close her performance). The transmission was so powerful, it is said, that Dame Nellie's voice was carried through the air to enthralled listeners all over Europe and as far away as Newfoundland.

In Christiania (now Oslo), the signal was so clear that a local wireless operator relayed the signal through the municipal telephone system, while in Paris a phonograph recording was made in the operations room beneath the Eiffel Tower.[11]

For all her pioneering spirit, though, Melba was a somewhat reluctant wireless adventurer. She had expressed disdain for Marconi's new wireless, pouring scorn on the public's appetite for these new 'magic playboxes', and things only seemed to get worse after she arrived at Marconi's studio in Chelmsford on the day of her transmission. During a tour of the broadcasting facility by the Marconi Company's chief publicist Arthur Burrows (who would go on to be a pioneer at the BBC), Melba was shown the giant transmitter masts looming over the works and informed that it was from there that her voice would be carried to listeners over distances of hundreds and even thousands

Test Match Special has been broadcast from the media centre at Lord's Cricket Ground in north London every summer since 1957.

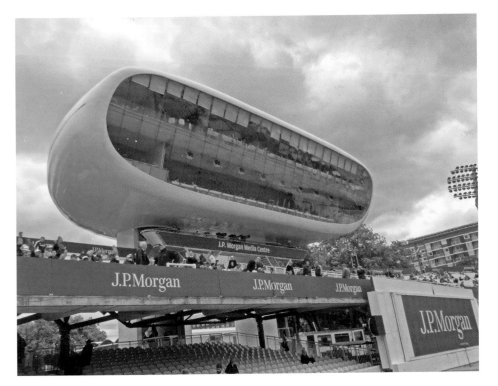

The distinctive 'indoor frame' of the superheterodyne radio receiver, 1925.

The UK's first all-transistor radio, the PAM 710, released in 1956.

The first 'boombox' was created by Phillips in 1966, but became synonymous with African American and Hispanic urban music in the U.S. from the mid-1970s, receiving the somewhat pejorative sobriquet 'ghetto blaster'.

of kilometres. Rather alarmed, Melba is reported to have said: 'Young man, if you think I am going to climb up there you are very much mistaken.'[12] In the end, Dame Nellie was a convert. She told the newspapers that the broadcast had been 'the most wonderful experience of my career', and the public appeared to agree. Letters arrived from all over the UK and Europe in the weeks and months that followed, commending the transmission. The transmission elevated Melba's status as prima donna par excellence still higher and was transformational in the public response to, and reputation of, wireless broadcasting. It had captured the imagination of the public and shown that wireless had the capacity to amuse, enthral and entertain.

The presence of music on the wireless in Britain did not, however, proceed smoothly. While radio executives in the U.S., such as the RCA founder David Sarnoff, equated radio to a 'music box', the rather more starchy and serious John Reith at the BBC insisted that broadcasting needed to strike a careful balance between emergent 'Reithean' principles: to educate, to inform and to entertain. Very different regulatory regimes in the UK and the U.S. (informed, among other things, by UK military fears that concerts and other 'frivolous' transmissions could jam vital strategic communications) ensured that wireless broadcasting in Britain and the United States developed along contrasting paths.

If music (and its relative neglect in the UK) played a part in defining very different institutional and regulatory environments for radio on either side of Atlantic, it would be the British public's appetite for a taste of American radio freedoms, and American music, that would be bring about another period of pioneering transformation in the 1960s. As we have already seen, British and European radio 'pirates' sought to overcome restrictive broadcasting regulations by transmitting their radio stations from ships anchored just beyond national territorial waters. While this was certainly an ideological mission, it was also one driven by a huge public demand for popular music on the radio waves. Unsurprisingly, the underlying politics and legal practices of broadcasting shaped and informed the status of radio very differently

Dame Nellie Melba and the BBC's 'matchbox' microphone, 1920.

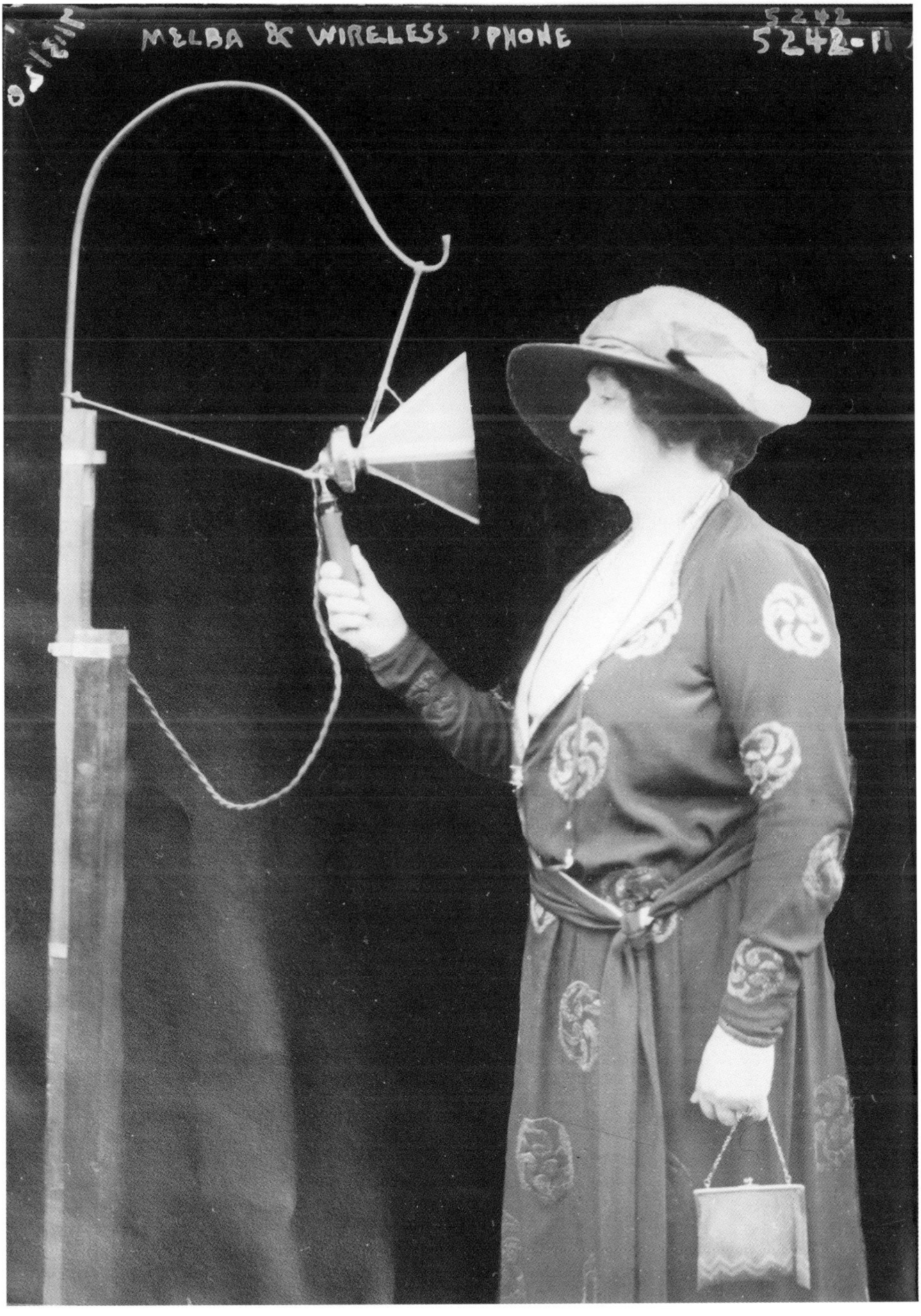

MELBA & WIRELESS PHONE

5242
5242-11

within U.S. and British popular culture. During the 1960s and '70s, for example, the great American songbook was filled with, as Stuart Maconie puts it, 'heartfelt hymns and incidental references to the joys of AM radio – from the Beach Boys to the Ramones, the Carpenters to Indeep's "Last Night a DJ Saved My Life!"'.[13] On the other hand, 'British pop songs about the radio come much later, are fewer in number and often take a distinctly ambivalent or cynical view.'[14] In the Carpenters' hit song 'Yesterday Once More' (1973), for example, the all-American duo recount the happiness and comforting familiarity of their youthful radio listening in Connecticut and, latterly, California.

Van Morrison's song 'In the Days before Rock 'n' Roll' (1990) is redolent of a British experience of music radio listening in the 1950s and early 1960s, when the limited musical offering available on the

Hollywood encounters the radio: silent movie star Clara Horton (1904–1976) listens to a musical concert on her radio receiver, 1925.

BBC's so-called Light Programme drove young listeners desperate to access popular music to European radio stations. Morrison invokes the spirit of his youthful self in a Northern Irish bedroom, furtively searching through radio stations from Ireland to Hungary in the hope of finding music that might inspire and entertain. Unlike in the U.S., hearing your favourite songs on the radio in Britain wasn't simply a case of waiting long enough; they had to be searched for and savoured because a signal could fade as quickly as it had been received. The poet Keith Burnett captures this sense of anticipation, excitement and loss in his poem '99.9 FM Radio Nostalgia', which was selected for inclusion in *Radio Waves*, an anthology of radio-related poetry from 2004. Invoking his childhood, Burnett recalls the sensation of his bed sheets burning his lips as Radio Luxembourg 'ran out of steam' and once again faded into 'a state of hiss'.[15]

The ascendency of the so-called 'radio pirates' would transform the British radio landscape and popular music culture in the UK. Their rise in the early 1960s, after all, not only prompted the Labour government of the day to hastily introduce the Marine Broadcasting Offences Act (1967) as a legislative mechanism to ensure the pirates' demise, but also a rather more pragmatic response from the BBC, which restructured its radio stations in order to create space for a newly formed pop music station, BBC Radio 1 (and employing many of the former pirates). Just as profoundly, though, the brief reign of the radio pirates seemed to spark a new wave of British musical creativity. 'Within eighteen months [of Radio Caroline's launch],' notes Simon Garfield, 'The Beatles, The Stones and The Who had thrown off not only post-war austerity and authority but also any notion that young people would ever be governable again.'[16]

Today, the combination of curated music and chat – the format that still sustains most popular-music stations around the world – remains immensely popular and is the subject of tremendous international competition. Whereas Radio 1 launched as a virtual monopoly for pop-music radio in 1967, today in the UK there are fifteen national radio stations on digital and or analogue platforms dedicated to pop and rock music – with upwards of another 250 regional and local radio stations doing likewise. A large proportion of these are commercial stations and are therefore supported with advertising revenue – although this has, itself, led to accusations that radio caters to a somewhat narrow, commercial musical taste. One such critique came in the form of the track 'Capital Radio' (1977) by the Clash, named for and released shortly after the launch of London's first commercial radio station. The song recalled the golden era of radio piracy and launched a stinging rebuke of this new radio station, whose policy of playing only mainstream chart hits (while ignoring the thriving 1970s punk scene) led the band to question the new station's claim to be 'in tune with London'.

Other song-makers have predicted the demise of radio due to a range of other social and technological factors. The British New Wave band The Buggles questioned whether radio could survive the visual onslaught of television and 'the VCR' in their first and only hit single, 'Video Killed the Radio Star', released in 1979. In an ironic twist for a song that laments the rise of the audio-visual, 'Video Killed the Radio Star' is now particularly well remembered as the very first music video to be screened on the then newly formed MTV in August 1981. Queen's 'Radio Ga Ga' (1984, written by the band's drummer Roger Taylor) expressed similar concerns, although radio's potential demise is made all the more poignant by memories of the nocturnal friendship radio offered during the band member's teenage years.

Radio – and perhaps music radio in particular – certainly has its challenges. Internet-based music-streaming services now have the capacity to curate very specific playlists based on the preferences of the listeners, effectively creating bespoke radio stations for each individual – although without, perhaps, the human intimacy that comes from radio listening in a more traditional sense. For many, these bespoke services contrast sharply with a concurrent tendency for commercial radio stations, especially in the United States, to become increasingly bland and generic in their output. Language provides a

Robin Williams (1951–2014) in character as AFN DJ Adrian Cronauer (1938–2018) in *Good Morning Vietnam.*

useful insight here. According to *Urban Dictionary*, the top definition for 'radio' today is:

A once novel concept completely and utterly destroyed by Clear Channel, which owns every radio station and only plays three shitty songs in steady rotation.[17]

Yet there is no convincing evidence that we are growing tired of radio. According to global figures gathered in 2015, 90 per cent of adults in the UK listen to the radio at least once a week, rising to 94 per cent in Sweden, 94 per cent in Poland and 98 per cent in China. In the United States, 76 per cent of adults listen at least once a week. Out of the countries surveyed, Poles listen to the most radio, averaging 32 hours per week, with Russians in second place (29 hours per week). By contrast Japanese, Australian and American listeners tune in for an average of fourteen hours per week. Advertising revenue on radio is also continuing to grow, which suggests that commercial radio will be around for some time to come.[18] Despite repeated talk of its demise, radio is proving to be the most adaptable and resilient of mediums, and continues to thrive even in an era of smartphones, tablets and Smart TVs. With record-high radio listenership recorded in the UK in 2016 and 2017, some have even suggested that radio may be experiencing a new 'golden age'. For Bob Shennan, the BBC's director of radio and music, this continuing success can be explained by radio's inherent qualities. 'It's very good at reaffirming its core values,' he noted in 2017, and remains, at least for now, 'the ultimate personalised service.'[19]

REFERENCES

INTRODUCTION

1 Ken Binmore and Paul Klemperer, 'The Biggest Auction Ever: The Sale of the British 3G Telecom Licences', *Economic Journal*, CXII/478 (2002), pp. C74–C96.

1 WIRELESS WORLDS

1 Helen Katz, *The Media Handbook: A Complete Guide to Advertising Media Selection, Planning, Research and Buying* (Mahwah, NJ, 2009).
2 Emily Thompson, *The Soundscape of Modernity: Architectural Acoustics and the Culture of Listening in America, 1900–1933* (Cambridge, MA, 2004), p. 301.
3 'The Temple of Sound', *Popular Mechanics* (December 1933), pp. 818–21. Also in Barry Blesser and Linda-Ruth Salter, 'Spaces Speak, Are You Listening?', in *Experiencing Aural Architecture*, ed. Barry Blesser and Linda-Ruth Salter (Cambridge, MA, 2006), p. 114.
4 'The New Tower of London', *Architectural Review*, LXXII/2, p. 43.
5 Margaret Hartmann, 'Sore Loser Rahm Emanuel Bashes One World Trade Center's "Antenna"', *New York Magazine*, www.nymag.com/intelligencer, 12 November 2013.
6 Peter Rejcek, 'Turn Up the Volume: McMurdo Radio Station Goes High-tech but Retains Retro Vinyl Collection', *Antarctic Sun*, https://antarcticsun.usap.gov/features, 24 February 2012.

7 'Underground Radio for Mine Rescues', *Popular Science Monthly* (April 1923).

8 Felice Cohen-Joppa, 'Project ELF Closes', *The Nuclear Resistor*, 135 (October 2004).

9 Shaun R. Gregory, *Nuclear Command and Control in NATO: Nuclear Weapons Operations and the Strategy of Flexible Response* (London and Basingstoke, 1996).

10 Paddy Scannell, *Radio, Television and Modern Life: A Phenomenological Approach* (Oxford, 1996), p. 165.

11 Terry Waite, *Taken on Trust* (London, 1993), p. 431.

12 David Hendy, *Radio in a Global Age* (London, 2000), p. 215.

13 Andrew Crisell, *Understanding Radio*, 2nd edn (New York, 1994), p. 3.

14 Alan Beck, 'Is Radio Blind or Invisible? A Call for a Wider Debate on Listening-in', *World Forum for Acoustic Ecology* (WFAE) (1999), www.wfae.proscenia.net, 22 August 2013; Alan Beck, 'Point-of-listening in Radio Plays', *Sound Journal* (1998), www.kent.ac.uk/arts/sound-journal, 22 August 2013.

2 MAKING WAVES

1 Tom Standage, *The Victorian Internet* (New York, 1998).

2 Lewis Mumford, *Technics and Civilization* (Chicago, IL, 2010), p. 89.

3 Maria Cristina Marconi, *Marconi My Beloved* (Boston, MA, 2001).

4 Erik Larsen, *Thunderstuck* (London, 2007), p. 122.

5 Vaclav Smil, *Creating the Twentieth Century: Technical Innovations of 1867–1914 and their Lasting Impact* (Oxford and New York, 2005).

6 H. C. Oersted, 'Experiments on the Effect of a Current of Electricity on the Magnetic Needle', *Annals of Philosophy*, XVI (1820), pp. 273–6.

7 Max Adams, *The Prometheans: John Martin and the Generation That Stole the Future* (London, 2013).

8 Geoffrey Hubbard, *Cooke and Wheatstone: And the Invention of the Electric Telegraph* (London, 1965).

9 Francis Ronalds, *Descriptions of an Electrical Telegraph: And of Some Other Electrical Apparatus* (London, 1823), pp. 2–3.

10 James Clerk Maxwell, 'A Dynamical Theory of the Electromagnetic Field', *Philosophical Transactions of the Royal Society of London*, CLV, (1865), p. 499.

11 Paul J. Nahin, *The Science of Radio: With Matlab and Electronics Workbench Demonstrations* (New York, 2001).

12 Andrew Norton et al., eds, *Dynamic Fields and Waves* (Milton Keynes, 2000), p. 83.

13 Oliver Heaviside, *Electromagnetic Theory* (New York, 2007), p. 5.

14 'Electrical Show', *New York Times* (15 May 1898), p. 10.

15 'Invented by Tesla – A Device That May Render Fleets and Guns Useless', *Middleton Daily Argus* (22 November 1898), p. 2.

16 Benjamin Franklin Miessner, *On the Early History of Radio Guidance* (San Francisco, CA, 1964).

17 W. Bernard Carlson, *Tesla: Inventor of the Electrical Age* (Princeton, NJ, 2013).

18 'Electricity at the Garden', *New York Times* (22 May 1898), p. 9.

19 Daniel Blair Stewart, *Tesla: The Modern Sorcerer* (Berkeley, CA, 1999), p. 371.

20 John W. Klooster, *Icons of Invention: The Makers of the Modern World from Gutenberg to Gates* (Santa Barbara, CA, 2009), p. 161.

21 'M. Marconi and the Ether Age', *South Wales Daily News* (23 May 1899), p. 6.

22 Rowland Pocock, *The Early British Radio Industry* (Manchester and New York, 1998).

23 W. J. Baker, *A History of the Marconi Company, 1874–1965* (Abingdon, 2002).

24 Sungook Hong, *Wireless: From Marconi's Black-box to the Audion* (Cambridge, MA, 2001).

25 Jill Hills, *The Struggle for Control of Global Communication: The Formative Century* (Urbana and Chicago, IL, 2002), p. 107.

26 J. A. Fleming, letter: 'Wireless Telegraphy', *The Times* (3 April 1899), p. 6.

27 B.F.S. Baden-Powell, letter: 'Wireless Telegraphy and War', *The Times* (5 April 1899), p. 9

28 Caroline Van Hasselt, *High Wire Act: Ted Rogers and the Empire that Debt Built* (Mississauga, ON, 2010).

29 'Maj. Armstrong, Radio Inventor, Plunges to Death', *The Post-Standard* (2 February 1954), p. 1.

3 RADIO AND THE NATION

1 FCC (2018) 'Broadcast Station Totals as of September 30, 2018', www.fcc.gov/document/broadcast-station-totals-september-30-2018.

2 Benedict Anderson, *Imagined Communities: Reflections on the Origin and Spread of Nationalism* (London, 1996), p. 56.

3 L. Claude Willcox, 'Amateurs' Experiences: Experimental Wireless Station at Warminster', *Wireless World*, II/14 (1914), p. 103.

4 Maurice Durieux, 'The CQ Serenade' (1951).

6 De Forest, advertisement: 'How Many Miles Did You Go Last Night?', *Radio Broadcast*, 1924, pp. 194–5.

7 Radiola, advertisement: 'Yay – A Touchdown!', *Popular Science Monthly*, December 1924, inside cover.

8 Radiola, advertisement: *Chicago Tribune*, 18 April 1926, p. 13.

9 Crosley, advertisement: 'Of Course it's a Crosley', *Popular Science Monthly*, December 1924, p. 1.

10 De Forest, 'How Many Miles'.

11 Ibid.

12 Donald Bogle, *Primetime Blues: African Americans on Network Television* (New York, 2001), p. 27.

13 Anson Rabinbach and Sander L. Gilman, *The Third Reich Sourcebook* (Berkeley and Los Angeles, CA, 2013), p. 615.

14 Albert Speer, quoted in Aldous Huxley, *Brave New World Revisited*, (New York, 1958), p. 37.

15   Marshall McLuhan, 'Radio: The Tribal Drum', *AV Communication Review*, XII/2 (1964), p. 143.

15   Ibid., pp. 14 and 139.

16   R. Murray Schafer, 'Acoustic Space', *Circuit*, XVII/3 (2007), pp. 83–6.

17   Hilmes and Loviglio, *Radio Reader: Essays in the Cultural History of Radio* (Abingdon, 2002).

18   Marshall McLuhan, 'Radio: The Tribal Drum'.

19   Amos Oz, *A Tale of Love and Darkness* (London, 2005), p. 342.

20   Tamar Liebes, 'Acoustic Space: The Role of Radio in Israeli Collective History', *Jewish History*, XX/1 (2006), p. 79.

21   Amos Oz, *A Tale of Love and Darkness*, p. 343.

22   Matt Mason, *The Pirate's Dilemma: How Youth Culture is Reinventing Capitalism* (New York, 2008), p. 41.

4 EMPIRES OF THE AIR

1   David Hendy, 'The Dreadful World of Edwardian Wireless', in *Moral Panics, Social Fears and the Media: Historical Perspectives*, ed. Siân Nicholas and Tom O'Malley (London, 2013), p. 78.

2   Joy Elizabeth Hayes, *Radio Nation: Communication, Popular Culture, and Nationalism in Mexico* (Tucson, AZ, 2000).

3   David Harvey, *The Condition of Postmodernity: An Enquiry into the Origins of Cultural Change* (Oxford, 1989); David Hendy, 'The Essay: Rewiring the Mind', BBC Radio 4, first broadcast June 2010.

4   Wim Vanobbergen, '"The Marvel of Our Time": Visions surrounding the Introduction of Radio Broadcasting in Belgium in the Radio Magazine "Radio" (1923–28)', *Media History*, XVI/2 (2010), pp. 199–213.

5   Brian Winston, *Media Technology and Society, A History: From the Telegraph to the Internet* (London, 1998).

6   James Wood, *History of International Broadcasting* (London, 2000), vol II, p. 110.

7   Margaret Fisher, 'New Information regarding the Futurist Radio
    Manifesto' (2011), *Italogramma*, I.

8   Filippo Marinetti, 'The Radio', in *Critical Writings: F. T. Marinetti*,
    ed. Gunter Berghaus (New York, 2006), p. x.

9   Neil Verma, *Theater of the Mind: Imagination, Aesthetics and American
    Radio Drama* (Chicago, IL, 2012), p. 25.

10 Gunter Berghaus, ed., *Filippo Tommaso Marinetti: Critical Writings*
    (New York, 2006), pp. 410–11.

11 Quoted in Emma Robertson, '"It is a Real Joy to get Listening
    of any Kind from the Homeland": BBC radio and British diasporic
    audiences in the 1930s', *Diasporas and Diplomacy: Cosmopolitan
    Contact Zones at the BBC World Service, 1932–2012*, ed. Marie Gillespie
    and Alban Webb (Abingdon, 2013), p. 27.

12 'London Day by Day: The King's Christmas Greeting', *Daily Telegraph*,
    27 December 1932, p. 6.

13 Simon J. Potter, *Broadcasting Empire: The BBC and the British World,
    1922–1970* (Oxford, 2012).

14 Marshall McLuhan, 'Radio: The Tribal Drum', *AV Communication
    Review*, XII/2 (1964), p. 143.

15 Ibid., pp. 14 and 139.

16 'A Message by His Majesty The King Broadcast to the Empire on
    Christmas Day 1932', *The BBC Year-book 1934* (London, 1934), p. 9.

17 Alasdair Pinkerton, 'Radio', in *The Ashgate Companion to Media
    Geography*, ed. Paul C. Adams et al. (Farnham, 2014), p. 60.

18 Douglas Kerr, 'In the Picture: Orwell, India and the BBC', *Literature
    and History*, XIII/1 (2004), pp. 43–57.

19 Zsolt Nagy, *Great Expectations and Interwar Realities: Hungarian
    Cultural Diplomacy* (Budapest, 2017).

20 César Saerchinger, 'Radio as a Political Instrument', *Foreign Affairs*,
    XVI/2 (January 1938), p. 249.

21 Callum A. MacDonald, 'Radio Bari: Italian Wireless Propaganda in
    the Middle East and British Countermeasures, 1934–1938', *Middle
    Eastern Studies*, XIII/2 (1977), p. 195.

22 Charles Rolo, *Radio Goes to War: The 'Fourth Front'* (New York, 1942), p. 41.

23 Rebecca Scales, *Radio and the Politics of Sound in Interwar France, 1921–1939* (Cambridge, 2016), p. 395.

24 Massimiliano Fiore, *Anglo-Italian Relations in the Middle East, 1922–1940* (Oxford, 2016), p. 41.

25 Frances S. Saunders, *Who Paid the Piper? The CIA and the Cultural Cold War* (London, 2000).

26 Richard H. Cummings, *Radio Free Europe's 'Crusade for Freedom': Rallying Americans behind Cold War Broadcasting, 1950–1960* (McFarland, CA, 2010).

27 Scott Lucas, *Freedom's War: The American Crusade Against the Soviet Union* (New York, 1999), p. 101.

5 RADIO WARS

1 Archibald Low, *Wireless Possibilities* (London, 1924), p. 64.

2 Ibid., p. 67.

3 Ibid., p. 71.

4 Ron Bartsch, James Coyne and Katherine Gray, *Drones in Society: Exploring the Strange New World of Unmanned Aircraft* (Abingdon, 2017).

5 'Thousands Flee Homes, Pray, or Faint as Fictitious Radio Program Relates Invasion by Martian Hordes', *Amarillo Globe-Times* (31 October 1938), p. 1.

6 Justone Levine, 'A History and Analysis of the Federal Communications Commission's Response to Radio Broadcast Hoaxes', *Federal Communication Law Journal*, LII/2 (2000), p. 279.

7 Gordon Allport and Hadley Cantril, *The Psychology of Radio* (London, 1935), p. vii.

8 Alden P. Armagnac, 'Weird Electrical Freaks Traced To Runaway Radio Waves', *Popular Science Monthly* CXXVI/5 (1935), p. 11.

9 Ibid., p. 268.

10 Ibid., p. 26.

11 Benedict Anderson, *Imagined Communities: Reflections on the Origin and Spread of Nationalism* (London, 1991).

12 Allport and Cantril, *The Psychology of Radio*, p. 3.

13 Keith Somerville, *Radio Propaganda and the Broadcasting of Hatred: Historical Development and Definitions* (London, 2010), p. 206.

14 ICTR (International Committee of the Red Cross), *The Media Case, The Prosecutor v. Ferdinand Nahimana, Jean-Bosco Barayagwiza, Hassan Ngeze* (2003), available at https://casebook.icrc.org.

15 David F. Channell, *A History of Technoscience: Erasing the Boundaries Between Science and Technology* (London, 2017).

16 David Haysom and Peter Jackson, *Covert Radar and Signals Interception: The Secret Career of Eric Ackermann* (Barnsley, 2000), pp. 8–9.

17 'Remarkable Radio Outfit Built By German Spy', *The Electrical Experimenter* (June 1917), p. 110.

18 Lewis Gullick, 'Espionage Battle Still Going On', *Eugene Register Guard* (15 December 1972).

6 RADIO AND POPULAR CULTURE

1 Ofcom, *The Communications Market Report* (16 December 2016), available at www.ofcom.org.uk.

2 Alan S. C. Ross, 'Linguistic Class-indicators in Present-day English', *Neuphilologische Mitteilungen*, LV/1 (1954), pp. 20–56.

3 Randall Jarrell, ed., *The Best Short Stories of Rudyard Kipling* (Garden City, NY, 1961), p. 403.

4 Roy Gibbons, 'Says New Radio Device Links the Living and the Dead', *Salina Daily Union* (17 May 1922), p. 7.

5 William Kalush and Larry Sloman, *The Secret Life of Houdini: The Making of America's First Superhero* (New York, 2007).

6 Sam Love, 'Radio Ghosts, Producing Music from Walls, Drive Off Tenants', *San Bernardino County Sun* (22 November 1928), p. 1.

7   Jeffrey Sconce, *Haunted Media* (Durham, NC, 2000), p. 68.

8   Alden P. Armagnac, 'Weird Electrical Freaks Traced To Runaway
    Radio Waves', *Popular Science Monthly*, CXXVI/5 (1935), p. 11.

9   Eric Zweig, 'Hockey Play-by-play was Born in Toronto 90 Years Ago',
    The Star, www.thestar.com (8 February 2013).

10 'Early Day Motion 1298, Test Match Special, Session: 2005–06',
    www.parliament.uk, July 2017.

11 Asa Briggs, *The History of Broadcasting in the United Kingdom*, vol. 1:
    The Birth of Broadcasting (Oxford, 1961), p. 43.

12 Sean Street, *A Concise History of British Radio, 1922–2002* (Tiverton,
    2002), p. 11.

13 Stuart Maconie, *The People's Songs: The Story of Modern Britain in
    50 Records* (London, 2014), p. 280.

14 Ibid.

15 Keith Burnett, '99.9 FM Radio Nostalgia', in *Radio Waves: Poems
    Celebrating the Wireless*, ed. Seán Street (London, 2004), p. 38.

16 Simon Garfield, *The Nation's Favourite: The True Adventures
    of Radio 1* (London, 1997).

17 'Radio', *Urban Dictionary*, www.urbandictionary.com, 8 November
    2003.

18 Ofcom, *The Communications Market Report, 3*: Radio and Audio
    (2016), available at www.ofcom.org.uk (accessed 19 July 2017).

19 Quoted in David Bond, '"Golden Age" for UK Radio as Number of
    Listeners Hits Record High', *Financial Times*, www.ft.com, 13 April
    2017.

SELECT BIBLIOGRAPHY

Anderson, Benedict, *Imagined Communities: Reflections on the Origin and Spread of Nationalism* (London, 1996)

Baker, W. J., *A History of the Marconi Company, 1874–1965* (Abingdon, 2002)

Bartsch, Ron, James Coyne and Katherine Gray, *Drones in Society: Exploring the Strange New World of Unmanned Aircraft* (Abingdon, 2017)

Briggs, Asa, *The History of Broadcasting in the United Kingdom*, vol. I: *The Birth of Broadcasting* (Oxford, 1961)

Cantril, Hadley, and Gordon Allport, *The Psychology of Radio* (London, 1935)

Carlson, W. Bernard, *Tesla: Inventor of the Electrical Age* (Princeton, NJ, 2013)

Channell, David F., *A History of Technoscience: Erasing the Boundaries Between Science and Technology* (London, 2017)

Garfield, Simon, *The Nation's Favourite: The True Adventures of Radio 1* (London, 1997)

Hayes, Joy Elizabeth, *Radio Nation: Communication, Popular Culture, and Nationalism in Mexico* (Tucson, AZ, 2000)

Haysom, David, and Peter Jackson, *Covert Radar and Signals Interception: The Secret Career of Eric Ackermann* (Barnsley, 2000)

Hendy, David, *Radio in a Global Age* (London, 2000)

Hong, Sungook, *Wireless: From Marconi's Black-box to the Audion* (Cambridge, MA, 2001)

Hubbard, Geoffrey, *Cooke and Wheatstone: And the Invention of the Electric Telegraph* (London, 1965)

Kalush, William, and Larry Sloman, *The Secret Life of Houdini: The Making of America's First Superhero* (New York, 2007)

Katz, Helen, *The Media Handbook: A Complete Guide to Advertising Media Selection, Planning, Research and Buying* (Mahwah, NJ, 2009).

Klooster, John W., *Icons of Invention: The Makers of the Modern World from Gutenberg to Gates* (Santa Barbara, CA, 2009)

Larsen, Erik, *Thunderstruck* (London, 2007)

McLuhan, Marshall, *Understanding Media: The Extensions of Man* (New York, 1964)

Maconie, Stuart, *The People's Songs: The Story of Modern Britain in 50 Records* (London, 2014)

Marconi, Maria Cristina, *Marconi My Beloved* (Boston, MA, 2001)

Miessner, Benjamin Franklin, *On the Early History of Radio Guidance* (San Francisco, CA, 1964)

Mumford, Lew, *Technics and Civilization* (Chicago, IL, 2010)

Nagy, Zsolt, *Great Expectations and Interwar Realities: Hungarian Cultural Diplomacy* (Budapest, 2017)

Nahin, Paul J., *The Science of Radio: With Matlab and Electronics Workbench Demonstrations* (New York, 2001)

Nicholas, Siân, and Tom O'Malley, eds, *Moral Panics, Social Fears and the Media: Historical Perspectives* (Abingdon, 2013)

Potter, Simon J., *Broadcasting Empire: The BBC and the British World, 1922–1970* (Oxford, 2012)

Rolo, Charles, *Radio Goes to War: The 'Fourth Front'* (New York, 1942)

Saunders, Frances S., *Who Paid the Piper? The CIA and the Cultural Cold War* (London, 2000)

Scales, Rebecca, *Radio and the Politics of Sound in Interwar France, 1921–1939* (Cambridge, 2016)

Scannell, Paddy, *Radio, Television and Modern Life: A Phenomenological Approach* (Oxford, 1999)

Sconce, Jeffrey, *Haunted Media* (Durham, NC, 2000)

Smil, Vaclav, *Creating the Twentieth Century: Technical Innovations of
    1867–1914 and their Lasting Impact* (Oxford and New York, 2005)
Somerville, Keith, *Radio Propaganda and the Broadcasting of Hatred:
    Historical Development and Definitions* (London, 2010)
Standage, Tom, *The Victorian Internet* (New York, 1998)
Stewart, Daniel Blair, *Tesla: The Modern Sorcerer* (Berkeley, CA, 1999)
Street, Sean, *A Concise History of British Radio, 1922–2002* (Tiverton, 2002)
Thompson, Emily, *The Soundscape of Modernity: Architectural Acoustics and
    the Culture of Listening in America, 1900–1933* (Cambridge and Boston,
    MA, 2004)
Waite, Terry, *Taken on Trust* (London, 1993)
Winston, Brian, *Media Technology and Society, A History: From the
    Telegraph to the Internet* (London, 1998)
Wood, James, *History of International Broadcasting*, vol. II (London, 2000)

ACKNOWLEDGEMENTS

This book is the product of research that began during my doctoral studies, sponsored by the Economic and Social Research Council, furthered under a British Academy Postdoctoral Fellowship and completed when a Reader in the Department of Geography at Royal Holloway, University of London. Throughout this time, I have been supported and guided by some wonderful colleagues within and beyond Royal Holloway, and sustained by lively discussions and debates with my incredible students.

I owe a particular debt of gratitude to my friends and family – especially my parents, brother and grandparents for their unceasing encouragement. My most heartfelt thanks go to Jamie and Will, who have already been subjected to more Radio 4 than is good for anyone, and to Philippa, my most tireless supporter and fiercest advocate. This book is dedicated to her in friendship and love.

PHOTO ACKNOWLEDGEMENTS

The author and publishers wish to express their thanks to the below sources of illustrative material and/or permission to reproduce it. Some locations are also given in the captions for the sake of brevity.

AP Photo/John Rooney: p. 173; photo © Father Browne/UIG/SSPL/Science and Society Picture Library – all rights reserved: p. 75; from the *Buffalo Police Department, Annual Report 1973* (Buffalo, NY, 1974): p. 163; photo by CBS via Getty Images: p. 183; photos © *Daily Herald* Archive/National Museum of Science and Media / Science and Society Picture Library – all rights reserved: pp. 13, 25, 40, 41, 69, 97, 101, 146, 149, 158, 188; David Rumsey Historical Map Collection (photo © 2018 Cartography Associates): p. 82; photo Orlando Fernandez/Library of Congress, Washington, DC (Prints and Photographs Division – New York World-Telegram and the Sun Newspaper Photograph Collection): p. 37; photo Mike Fitzpatrick, reproduced by kind permission: p. 170; from *Gastonia Daily Gazette*, 3 November 1938: p. 143; photos Carol M. Highsmith/Library of Congress, Washington, DC (Prints and Photographs Division – Carol M. Highsmith Archive): pp. 24, 27; from *Ladies' Home Journal* (December 1930): p. 94; photos Library of Congress, Washington, DC (Prints and Photographs Division): pp. 6, 13, 51, 61, 70, 76, 84, 85, 136, 140, 204; photos Library of Congress, Washington, DC (Prints and Photographs Division – George Grantham Bain Collection): pp. 95, 167, 203; photos Library of Congress, Washington, DC (Prints and Photographs Division – Harris and Ewing Collection): pp. 78, 117, 151; photo

if changes were made – you may do so in any reasonable manner, but not in any way that suggests the licensor endorses you or your use; and you may not apply legal terms or technological measures that legally restrict others from doing anything the license permits.

INDEX